POLITICS AND SOCIAL THEORY

Edited by Peter Lassman
Lecturer, Department of Political Science
and International Studies
University of Birmingham

Published under the auspices of the
British Sociological Association

R

ROUTLEDGE
London and New York

First published in 1989 by
Routledge
11 New Fetter Lane, London EC4P 4EE
29 West 35th Street, New York NY 10001

© 1989 British Sociological Association

Phototypeset in 10pt Times by
Mews Photosetting, Beckenham, Kent
Printed and bound in Great Britain by Mackays of Chatham PLC, Kent

British Library Cataloguing in Publication Data

Politics and social theory
    1. Politics. Theories
    I. Lassman, Peter
    320′.01
    ISBN 0-415-01799-8

Library of Congress Cataloging in Publication Data also available
ISBN 0-415-01799-8

Contents

Contributors

R.N. Berki is Professor of European Political and Social Theory and Head of the Department of European and Modern Dutch Studies at the University of Hull. Among his publications are *The History of Political Thought: a Short Introduction* (1977), *On Political Realism* (1981), *Insight and Vision: The Problem of Communism in Marx's Thought* (1983), and *Security and Society: Reflections on Law, Order and Politics* (1986).

John F. Bird is senior lecturer in Sociology at Bristol Polytechnic. He has written a number of papers on the works of Foucault with reference to the sociologies of health and illness. A study of nineteenth-century asylum casebooks is being prepared for publication under the title *Women, Madness and Marginality*.

Nancy Fraser teaches philosophy, women's studies and comparative literature and theory at Northwestern University. She has published widely on feminist theory, neo-marxian social theory, postmodernism and the politics of literary theory. *Unruly Practices: Power, Discourse and Gender in Late-Capitalist Social Theory* is forthcoming (1988).

Barry Hindess is Professor of Sociology at the Australian National University. He is the author of several books on contemporary political and social theory including *Parliamentary Democracy and Socialist Politics* (1983), *Freedom, Equality and the Market* (1986), *Politics and Class Analysis* (1987), and *Choice and Rationality in Social Theory* (1988).

Wayne Hudson is senior lecturer in the School of Humanities at Griffith University. He is the author of *The Marxist Philosophy of Ernst Bloch* (1982) as well as of numerous papers on modern social and political philosophy.

Peter Lassman is lecturer in Political Science at the University of

Birmingham. He is the coeditor of *Max Weber's 'Science as a Vocation'* (1988) as well as of several papers on modern social and political theory. Currently working on Weber and on critiques of liberalism.

Christopher Pierson is lecturer in Political Studies, Sociology and Social Policy at the University of Stirling. He has published several papers on social and political theory as well as *Marxist Theory and Democratic Politics* (1987). He is currently engaged in research on the comparative development of the welfare state.

Göran Therborn is Professor of Sociology at Gothenburg University. His publications include *Science, Class and Society* (1976), *The Ideology of Power and the Power of Ideology* (1981) and *Why Some Peoples are More Unemployed than Others* (1986). He is finishing a book on *The Political Sociology of Human Reproduction* and another (in Swedish) on *The Making of the Swedish Bourgeoisie*.

Irving Velody is lecturer in Sociology at the University of Durham. He is coeditor of the interdisciplinary journal *History of the Human Sciences* and of *Max Weber's 'Science as a Vocation'* (1988). He is currently working on problems concerning the internal logic of sociological theory.

Preface

The essays collected here are, with one exception, based upon papers delivered at a conference of the British Sociological Association Theory Group held at the University of Birmingham on the 12th and 13th of September 1985. This conference was part of a series that had taken as its general theme an exploration of the 'boundaries of sociology'.

This topic proved to be a very popular one attracting a large number of participants and many offers of papers. I would like to apologize to all who offered excellent papers that I was not able to include. Limitations of time and space were alone responsible for the refusal of papers. I would like to thank all who attended the conference as well as the authors of the essays that appear here.

Many people gave me support in organizing the conference and in getting this volume off the ground. Mike Milotte of the BSA played a crucial role in the whole project. I was also fortunate in having the advice of David Perman who had organized an earlier conference on the theme of 'Sociology and Economics'.

Peter Lassman

Chapter one

Introduction: Politics and Social Theory

Peter Lassman

The title page of the first edition of Durkheim's *The Division of Labour in Society* contains the following quotation from Aristotle's *Politics*: 'A state (*polis*) is not made up of only so many men, but of different kinds of men, for similars do not constitute a state' (Aristotle 1984:2001).

It is an interesting fact in itself that Durkheim chose to quote this text for in doing so several things are indicated. Firstly, and obviously, that he was a student of the classical literature of political philosophy and saw its relevance for his own project of creating a social science. He also recognized the centrality for social theory of the problem of reconciling plurality and order within a complex society. In making this observation it is important to note that all of the 'founders' of modern social theory were conscious of the reversal that they were effecting in the classical understanding of politics. It is a mark of their success in effecting what was an almost total transformation in thought that it is so little remarked upon. Translated into modern terms a central topic for social theory has always been the problem of the relationship between the 'state' and 'society'. There is, at the heart of modern social theory, an attempt to supplant the language of classical political philosophy in favour of a new language, conceived in various forms, of science. The predicament of contemporary social theory constructed in the scientific mode follows from the fact that, although this is far from being universally recognized, the confidence that a 'science of the social' could ever be constructed has been systematically undermined. Without going into the way in which the development of modern philosophy has contributed to this state of affairs it is important to recognize that the idea of a social science in the form presented by the mainstream tradition of modern sociology from Comte to Parsons, and, probably, Habermas too, has been open to fundamental criticism in its claim to present an objective account of the social realm.

The claim to present a picture of society that aspires to the status of a scientific theory must mean that no area of social life is immune from its explanatory claims. Clearly, on this account, the realm of politics and of the political must be as amenable to social scientific explanation

1

as is any other area of human affairs. The assumption that is being made here is that the 'political' simply *is* a constituent part, or in modern terms, a subsystem, of something called 'society'. This is the fundamental assumption of practically all modern social science and this includes much of what is called 'political science' too. There is a fundamental conflict of interpretation here between the language of political philosophy, the language of the *polis*, and the language of 'society' conceived as an order that encompasses the political sphere.

What is at issue here is the very concept of 'the political' that is being taken for granted in the discourse of modern social theory. The typical approach of the contemporary social scientist appears to be an assertion that all that is required to keep up with the times is to pay more attention to the question of the 'role of the state' and to the problem of power. However, from the standpoint of a more classical attitude this line of argument is still imprisoned within a way of thinking that has distinct limitations. Thus, in a manner that is typical of the modern form of social science, when Durkheim quotes Aristotle he ignores or perhaps 'creatively misreads' him. It is in this way that all those questions raised by the classical notion of politics are sublimated into a new form of discourse. In the classical view 'politics' does not refer simply to the institutions of government and of domination but is regarded as being an essential part of all the important aspects of the shared life of a community (Sartori 1973; Wolin 1985). In the modern social scientific view 'the political' is a separate department of 'society' and it is such that its operation is subsumable by those general laws or processes that are presumed to operate throughout its structure.

Even more remote from most of modern social science is that other aspect of the Aristotelian science of politics which is the idea of 'the political' as that science which is concerned with the 'good for man'. There has always been a tension here in the work of modern social scientists. On the one hand, they are, in differing ways, committed to the idea of creating an objective as possible scientific account while, on the other hand, their motivation for constructing such a science in the first place is irreducibly 'value laden' and, hence, ultimately political in character. It has long been a commonplace in the interpretation of the history of the emergence of modern social science to point out that it was from its origins a 'crisis science', a reflection of its own times. For all its rhetorical use of claims to scientificity the discourse of the social sciences cannot escape from the fact that it itself exists within the political realm and, hence, cannot escape from the fate of being a political discourse. Even when its subject matter is not political in content its explanatory concepts rely upon notions of human nature and of 'what is good for man' and these concepts are themselves of an essentially contestable character (Taylor 1967). Such explanatory structures are far from possessing any of the characteristics that are normally assumed to be those of a genuine science. They are, in fact, derived from political philosophies in the traditional sense. Indeed it has been argued convincingly that given the collapse of the 'positivist' notion of scientific explanation and the recognition of the importance of the idea that all theories are underdetermined with regard to fact, it follows that in the social sciences

> the proposal of a social theory is more like the arguing of a political case than like a natural-science explanation. It should seek for and respect the facts when these are to be had, but it cannot await a possibly unattainable total explanation. It must appeal explicitly to value judgements and may properly use persuasive rhetoric. (Hesse 1978)

If we accept this argument then we are clearly back in the traditional territory of political justification and of political judgement.

The explicit distinction between 'state' and 'society' is a product of a fairly recent intellectual development. It seems that it was Hegel who first systematically developed the distinction between 'civil society' and the 'state'. In Hegel's account the two spheres are interdependent but it is the state that is the highest form of human association. The relevant point here is that Hegel still takes the state to be logically more fundamental than society and it is on this very point that there is a fundamental difference of opinion between the mainstream of the tradition of western political philosophy and that of the modern form of social science. The fundamental assumption of the social scientific outlook is that 'society' is the foundation for the 'state' and that the 'social' existence of human beings is more fundamental than is their political existence. It is on this point that, for example, both Marx and Durkheim agree. Here, despite all the differences between them in terms of method, the nature of industrial society or of the function of the state, they operate with the common assumption that man is essentially a 'social', rather than a 'political' being. It is instructive to note that they both dismiss Aristotle in similar terms. In Durkheim's view Aristotle is simply pre-scientific; his 'classification of societies tells us nothing about their nature' (Durkheim 1960:9). Similarly, Marx from his earliest writings is concerned to reverse the traditional view of the relationship between the 'state' and 'society'. This aspect of Marx's thought is well known but it is worth stressing the fact that he never changed his opinion on this point and that it is of fundamental importance for his whole outlook. In *Capital* he asserts that 'man is, if not as Aristotle contends, a political, at all events a social animal' (Marx 1961:326). Durkheim would not have disagreed.

Among the 'classical' theorists Max Weber, as one would expect, is a much more complex thinker to categorize in these terms. Nevertheless, any attempt to consider his fundamental 'thema' in terms of its

derivation from political philosophy must still face the difficulty of reconciling those elements in his thought that are consistent with that interpretation with those that are not (Hennis 1983). Among these latter
features there is, most obviously, his denial of the relevance of the classics
for an understanding of the modern world and his redefinition of the
sphere of politics in terms of the apparatus of the modern state, which,
in turn, is identified with the struggle for power and nothing else. Of
course, the seeds of this view were sown from within the political
philosophical tradition itself but it is still true to assert that it is here
that there exists a fundamental difference of outlook between the two
opposing languages of the state and of the nature of politics (Wolin 1960).
When Marx made this idea central to his own thought he made it
impossible for any marxist to produce an enlightening theory of politics
without so seriously revising the views of the master that in doing so
all that is distinctive of marxism as a theory is removed. All attempts
to appeal to a supposedly more 'sociological' or more 'realistic' Marx
who can contribute to the creation of a theory of the modern state that
would be plausible for contemporary social scientists cannot overcome
this barrier. Such revisions can only appeal either to some rather scat-
tered remarks in his more marginal writings, or to meaningless notions
such as those of the state's supposed possession of 'relative autonomy'.

The consolidation of the 'social science paradigm' coincided with a
period in which the traditional activity of political philosophy appeared
to have exhausted itself. There was a general mood in which it was
assumed that the traditional problems were for the most part meaningless
and that empirically minded social sciences were the rightful successors
to these now discredited disciplines. Today, we live in a different world.
The confidence in the ability of the social sciences to explain and to
understand has been seriously eroded while there has been a considerable
revival in the fortunes of political philosophy. It is no longer considered
to be a marginal activity and although much recent writing in political
philosophy does draw upon work done in the social sciences and
especially in economics and political science it is nevertheless recognized as being a legitimate and autonomous province of enquiry.
Meanwhile, as mentioned above, the centrality and unavoidability of
questions of value within all of the social sciences can no longer be denied
with conviction.

There is a highly persuasive thesis that argues that the transition to
a distinctively social form of theory is a mark of the decline of the sense
of the 'political' in western thought. This thesis has, above all, been
associated with the work of writers such as Arendt and Wolin who, in
different ways, have attempted to reconstruct the history of social and
political thought (Wolin 1960; Arendt 1958). However, it must be
remarked that there is a history of scepticism concerning the self-
interpretation of the social sciences that has existed for as long as

they have. Even if the true history of this development is much more untidy than it is often presented (and it is probably impossible to be precise about any presumed transition from one discourse to another simply because several competing discourses have coexisted) it still remains true to say that there has been a profound shift in our conceptual vocabulary (Collini, Winch and Burrow 1983). The real question here is one of the status of politics and of the political in our understanding of the modern world. Wolin has stated the problem in a succinct manner:

> When modern social science asserts that political phenomena are to be explained by resolving them into sociological, psychological, or economic components, it is saying that there are no distinctively political phenomena and hence no special set of problems. (Wolin 1960:288)

The essays collected in this book are all in their various ways a reflection of the predicament of contemporary social and political analysis. Although they are written from different intellectual, disciplinary and political perspectives they all address themselves to the problem of how the 'political' is to be understood within a context in which the old certainties of the social sciences are not only felt to be inadequate for an understanding of the contemporary world but, more fundamentally, it is now being asserted more openly than ever before that the entire modern project for the construction of a social science was fatally flawed from the start. The interpretation of industrialism, once thought to be its greatest claim on our attention, is now shown to be historically naive. Further, there are good epistemological reasons for believing that such theories could never be as adequate as they were originally assumed to be. As one recent survey of the entire field gloomily concludes,

> [the] history of the twentieth century is one in which passions and interests have remained defiantly particular, and in so far as they are public, have remained so in good part for political rather than social reasons, it is scarcely surprising that as the theories they were intended to be these theories have failed us, have come in many cases to cease to connect to *us* at all. (Hawthorn 1987:275)

The problem here is that a boundary of the 'social' has always been provided by 'politics'. It is an unavoidable fact that the attempt to do 'social science' must imply a denial of the centrality of the political domain. This, of course, is an impossibility. We live in a political world. Hence, despite all denials and attempts to be 'value free' and to avoid discussion of the political implications of social science political ideas and political judgements creep in through the back door. In a world that is itself politically constituted the denial of politics is itself a political phenomenon. When modern social scientists argue for the recognition of the growth of the activities of the state and of the 'politicization' of social relations then they must also recognize that they are exchanging the certainties of science for the unpredictability of politics (Sartori 1969:214).

In the first essay Berki examines the coexistence of three languages or vocabularies of the state. There are in existence three autonomous languages: the philosophical, the literary and the social scientific. That the philosophical and the social scientific languages continue as rival accounts of the field is an interesting feature of the intellectual landscape. The rise of scientific enquiry does not and can never eliminate philosophy, least of all in the field of political and social enquiry. Berki proposes that the only way to make sense of this is to regard these languages as being complementary and mutually reinforcing. But what is important for the social scientist to note is that no amount of investigation or even of 'progress' in these fields will eliminate the necessity for the philosophical vocabulary. There is an endless process of argument and counterargument in which none of the three languages can either disappear or have the last word.

The transition to the modern concept of 'society' is an essential part of Marx's intellectual achievement. However, as often appears to be the case, such advances are made at a price. The price that marxism has paid since its foundation has been its weak sense of politics and of the state. In asserting the primacy of 'civil society' Marx was unable to see the reality of the state and of the political as being anything other than an aspect of human self-alienation. The problem that is the focus of Pierson's essay is the problem faced by all attempts to create a political theory of the modern state whether it be 'capitalist' or 'socialist'. As he notes, there is a 'pervasive characteristic' of marxist thought to see all politics as class politics. Clearly, in the modern world of 'new social movements' and of major political struggles that have no significant class basis this is an inadequate standpoint to maintain. Most worrying for contemporary marxian theorizing is the existence of 'actually existing socialism' in which the state shows no sign of either 'withering away' or of being transcended and from which politics can never be completely removed. The interesting and new development here is the way in which there has been a recognition on the left that many of the criticisms of marxism that were formerly characterized as products of the 'cold war', such as those of Popper and Talmon, ought not to be so easily dismissed (Popper 1945; Talmon 1960). In other words, the central problem that emerges here is the traditional one of reconciling socialism with freedom. Can there be a democratic socialism? If there is to be a return to a recognition of the 'necessity of politics' in a 'pluralist socialism' then this is clearly a return to a central topic of traditional political theory which Marx himself and most 'orthodox' marxists thought of as belonging to an 'ideological' and pre-marxist past.

The social analysis of politics has rested, for most theoretical schools, upon ideas of social class. In an essay of radical 'deconstruction' Hindess seeks to show that this is a major defect of modern social and political thought rather than being, as it is usually assumed to be, a strength. Hindess' claim is to go beyond the necessity of avoiding reductionism in showing that the very idea of social classes as being 'social forces' is itself incoherent. The fundamental difficulty here is the assumption that social classes can be conceived as 'collective actors' in any useful sense and that as collective entities they possess objectively given collective interests by virtue of their position in the overall structure of society. To talk of social classes in this way is clearly, on this account, to commit a 'category mistake'. It is not even clear what it would mean to talk of classes 'making decisions' even when this is recognized as a piece of metaphorical redescription. It is an important part of Hindess's argument to show that these conceptual confusions are not the private property of marxian analyses alone, as one might be led to expect. In fact, they run right through the mainstream of contemporary social theory. Using the example of recent studies of social mobility he shows how, despite their professed claim to put this topic in a wider political perspective, they completely fail to take account of 'real' political actors such as political parties, trade unions, and the state. To do so would, of course, introduce an element of political unpredictability, of 'fortuna', that would sit uneasily with the heavy investment in modern research technology (MacIntyre 1972). In fact, according to Hindess contemporary analysis seems to work with two levels of analysis; one is an account of the political realm, the other is of a clash of 'mythical beasts'. The seemingly insoluble problem is to combine the 'irreducibility of politics with the explanatory promise of reductionism'. Readers of refined accounts of contemporary social theory will recognize here a version of their old friends the so-called dualisms of 'action and structure' and of 'system and structure'.

A set of common themes run through the remaining essays linking them together despite the differences in their subject matter. Modernity, welfare, new social movements and structures of power are central topics of contemporary social and political theory. It seems to be in the nature of these phenomena that they both raise new problems and, at the same time, lead to the reconsideration of old ones. As Therborn argues, the expansion of the activity of the state is a central feature of the modern world and yet it is a development that is still awaiting an adequate explanation. Looking at the modern welfare state in particular it is clear that there is no obvious nor generally accepted explanation of its progress and character. The diversity of national experiences implies that no evolutionary account is likely to succeed while narratives, such as that of T.H. Marshall, based upon the experience of one state, do not travel well and cannot form the foundation for a comparative investigation of other European states. If all modern states are subject to similar sets of problems it does not follow that they perceive them in identical ways nor that their political responses are identical. The desire for understanding on a comparative scale founders on the reef of historical particularity which, in this case, must include forms of political understanding and of judgement.

An emerging theme in political discourse is the question of 'modernity'. Despite the obscurity, confusion and vagueness that attaches itself to this term, as Hudson points out, its use does point to a range of important questions. If, as Lyotard and others argue, it is true to say that the 'grand metanarratives' are in retreat then fundamental problems are raised about the nature of politics in a 'post-modern' world (Lyotard 1984). How do new political movements define themselves? How do political regimes claim legitimacy in the absence of such 'metanarratives'? One emerging theoretical approach, or more accurately, set of approaches is that of modern feminism. Feminist political theory has brought back into the central arena of debate the reconsideration of fundamental categories of political discourse. In the context of an analysis of the American system of social welfare Nancy Fraser shows how the whole debate about welfare raises questions of a distinctly political character. In so far as the operation of the welfare state rests upon concepts of 'need', then, conflicts over the interpretation of 'need', which are political arguments, are inevitable. The merit of the feminist critique here is to show that there is an unavoidable requirement to reassess fundamental political categories such as the public/private distinction and that the whole area of 'social welfare' discourse is an irreducibly political domain. In Fraser's view the rise of the 'social' is a mark of modernity but *pace* Arendt this is not a sign of decline but of a positive development. Indeed it is of fundamental importance for most feminist accounts that the public/private distinction becomes blurred and that it is recognized that those areas formerly thought of as belonging to the private sphere be shown to be the proper objects for public debate. Thus 'needs' are not 'natural' nor are they 'private' but are 'social' and, therefore, 'subject to critique and contestation'.

The 'politics of need interpretation' links the topic of the welfare state with the 'discourse of modernity'. The work of Foucault occupies a central place in this debate. His writings are of obvious relevance to the questions raised by contemporary social and political theorists. As Bird shows very clearly Foucault, despite the currently fashionable nature of the reception of his work, is dealing with quite fundamental issues. Indeed, what could be more fundamental than the problem of the relationship between knowledge and politics? Foucault has become, almost paradoxically, a central figure in the debate about 'modernity' by discussing traditional problems. The additional element in his work of 'extending the questionnaire' to new areas is the way in which he has then made that the ground for examining those very problems. An example of this is the way in which he has extended the argument about the nature of power so that it can be argued that there is a definite 'politics of the body'. Of course, in so far as the body has 'needs' a distinctly new political discourse emerges. The problem with Foucault's approach in the eyes of many of his critics is that his 'microphysics' of power seems to undermine the attempt to construct 'general' theories or explanations and to point in the direction of a 'post-modernism' in which distinctions between the 'political' and the 'social' lose their relevance.

In making use of the concept of 'the essential copy', which is taken from the history of art, Velody shows how the projects of both modern sociology and socialism share common epistemological features. They both emerge from a common background in Enlightenment optimism and ideas of progress and science. Nevertheless they have often been regarded as competitors in the same explanatory game. Durkheim, for example, certainly felt that he had to explain away the claims made by socialism to be offering an alternative scientific account of society. Clearly, the attempt to treat socialism as just another 'social fact' was an attempt to undermine its political ambitions. The use of a rhetoric of science in the claims to knowledge made by both socialism and sociology can be regarded as being no more than a device that hides the essentially political nature of this debate. Even Weber, whose intellectual stance is totally unlike that of Durkheim, cannot admit that his discussion of socialism is much more like an essay in political theory than a statement of social science. What is relevant for the discussion here is that both mainstream sociology and socialism share the common failing that in their eyes political activity must appear to play 'a subordinate, not to say ephemeral role'. The epistemological foundations of both sociology and socialism have been on the receiving end of some highly damaging criticism. The most recent form that this has taken has revolved around the idea that there is a specifically 'post-modern' condition that culminates in the erosion of those 'metanarratives' upon which such 'modern' projects as sociology and socialism must be founded.

The problem with all talk about 'modernity' and 'post-modernity' is its inherent vagueness and ambiguity. As Hudson makes it abundantly clear, there seems to be a deep (modern?) need to clarify the idea of a 'post-modern condition'. What is of most relevance here is the question of whether it makes sense at all to talk of a set of specifically 'post-modern' political questions. A central theme in the political debate is the question of a presumed crisis of authority and of legitimation. It is probably best to regard the concepts of the 'modern' and of the 'post-modern' as performing a role similar to that of the topics of classical rhetoric rather than as being scientific 'super concepts'. In this sense, these concepts have played an important role in alerting us to a recognition of the importance of new questions, developing new debates and reviving old ones. Thus in the current discussion on the nature of 'post-modern' politics it has been argued that there is a fundamental problem concerning the 'legitimation' of the 'post-modern bourgeois liberal' regimes. In his critique of Lyotard, for example, Rorty has argued that such regimes, of which he approves, can only be defended on pragmatic grounds. The search for some 'metanarrative' of justification such as that presupposed by 'critical theory' in its Habermasian form or the search for an 'archimedian point' as in the work of Rawls are both mistaken (Rorty 1983, 1984).

Such considerations as these simply reinforce an important point that emerges from a reading of the essays collected here. This is simply that the map of the social sciences and the shifting lines of division between them is constantly changing and that the way that these changes occur is bound up with changes in social and political life itself. This point was recognized very clearly by Max Weber. Modern western society is increasingly becoming a 'political' society and under such conditions the centrality of political questions reasserts itself in a way that cannot be ignored. With the waning of the last remnants of the view that a science of society, when fully operational, would solve, abolish or sidestep the fundamental political questions that all complex societies must face, the traditional perception of these affairs necessarily reasserts itself. The classical tradition of sociology was a necessary 'moment' in the history of modern social and political thought but in its development it has generated a set of paradoxes and problems that it cannot resolve from within its own intellectual resources (Unger 1975, 1976). When modern social science is left to its own devices the result, too often, is a sterile formalism accompanied by a frenzied survey of the horizon of current events in search of new subject matter. The only escape is to recognize that the end of that tradition has arrived and although this does not mean that we will cease to learn from it, it does mean that we transcend it through a recognition that political understanding, which is neither science nor pure philosophy, is an essential and unavoidable component of all social inquiry.

References

Arendt, H. (1958) *The Human Condition*. Chicago: University of Chicago.
Aristotle (1984) *The Complete Works of Aristotle Vol 2*, (ed.) J. Barnes. Princeton: Princeton University Press.
Collini, S., Winch, D. and Burrow, J. (1983) *That Noble Science of Politics*. Cambridge: Cambridge University Press.
Durkheim, E. (1960) *Montesquieu and Rousseau: Forerunners of Sociology*.

Ann Arbor: University of Michigan Press.

Hawthorn, G. (1987) *Enlightenment and Despair: A History of Sociology*. Cambridge: Cambridge University Press.

Hennis, W. (1983) 'Max Weber's "Central Question"', *Economy and Society* 12:135–80.

Hesse, M. (1978) 'Theory and Value in the Social Sciences', in Christopher Hookway and Philip Pettit (eds) *Action and Interpretation: Studies in the Philosophy of the Social Sciences*. Cambridge: Cambridge University Press.

Lyotard, J.-F. (1984) *The Postmodern Condition*. Manchester: Manchester University Press.

MacIntyre, A. (1972) 'Is a Science of Comparative Politics Possible?', in Peter Laslett, W.G. Runciman and Quentin Skinner (eds) *Philosophy, Politics and Society. Fourth Series*. Oxford: Basil Blackwell.

Marx, K. (1961) *Capital Vol 1*. London: Lawrence & Wishart.

Popper, K. (1945) *The Open Society and its Enemies*. London: Routledge & Kegan Paul.

Rorty, R. (1983) 'Postmodernist Bourgeois Liberalism', *The Journal of Philosophy* 80 (10):583–9.

Rorty, R. (1984) 'Habermas and Lyotard on Postmodernity', *Praxis International* 4(1):32–44.

Sartori, G. (1969) 'From the Sociology of Politics to Political Sociology', *Government and Opposition* 4:195–214.

Sartori, G. (1973) 'What is Politics?' *Political Theory* 1(1):5–26.

Talmon, J.L. (1960) *The Origins of Totalitarian Democracy*. New York: Praeger.

Taylor, C. (1967) 'Neutrality in Political Science', in Peter Laslett and W.G. Runciman, (eds) *Philosophy, Politics and Society. Third Series*. Oxford: Basil Blackwell.

Unger, R.M. (1975) *Knowledge and Politics*. New York: The Free Press.

Unger, R.M. (1976) *Law in Modern Society*. (New York: The Free Press.

Wolin, S.S. (1960) *Politics and Vision*. Boston: Little, Brown & Co.

Wolin, S.S. (1985) 'Postmodern Politics and the Absence of Myth', *Social Research* 52(2):217–39.

Chapter two

Vocabularies of the State

R.N. Berki

The modern state, as everybody agrees, is rather a baffling phenomenon. The concept itself is a prime example of what philosophers often call 'essentially contestable' concepts. What is the state, really? Is it, essentially and primarily, a kind of paternal agency, the family writ large, a gathering of like-minded friends who are in the habit of accepting the same rules of conduct? Is it an association to be defined primarily in terms of force, a cold and impersonal entity oppressing the single individual? Or is it a contrivance, a network of offices and institutions, whose chief function is the adjustment of conflicting social interests? Most of us would probably tend to say 'yes' to all these three questions. The overall argument of this paper is that an affirmative answer to the three questions is, in fact, *correct* in each case, never mind the seeming incompatibility of the three images — scenarios, conceptual edifices, paradigms — conjured up by these questions themselves. We shall endeavour to show here that the modern state — though not perhaps 'all things to all men' — is at least three things to most people, and irreducibly so.

What we need, in order adequately to understand the essential character of the modern state, is what might be called a 'plural perspective', a kind of comprehension which, meeting the given paradox head-on, entertains three scenarios at the same time and accepts, up to a point, the validity of each. The three paradigms will be called here, respectively, the *philosophical*, the *literary*, and the *social-scientific* paradigm, for reasons which will become apparent later. The paradigms or perspectives to be discussed contain distinct, though not entirely self-enclosed, *vocabularies* or languages; hence the title of this paper. But the resemblance to two famous modern texts in political philosophy is not wholly fortuitous. T.D. ('Harry') Weldon's iconoclastic *Vocabulary of Politics* (1953), following on the more sedate *States and Morals*, set out to show that the 'state' (like other supposed 'solids' in political discourse) was nothing essentially: words are sign-posts for orientation. Michael Oakeshott's two seminal articles, 'The Vocabulary of a Modern European State' (*Political Studies*, 1975), argue that there are two prominent languages in politics: the language of authority and the language of power. This paper imitates, to a certain extent, Weldon's iconoclastic purpose but it adopts a more constructive, not to say traditional, approach to 'essentialism': we are arguing, not that the state is nothing essentially but that it has, in a manner of speaking, three irreducible essences. And our three paradigms, as readers familiar with Oakeshott's writings will note, are a further development (whether legitimate or not, from the strict orthodox Oakeshottian point of view) of Oakeshott's two 'languages'.

We shall start by briefly describing the three essential languages of the state, with their respective textual credentials, and then we shall attempt to construct them logically, showing how one leads to and is in some measure superseded by the other. In the last section of the paper an effort will be made to demonstrate irreducibility, i.e. that the apparently superseded languages, vocabularies still have a substantial presence in comprehension and discourse; not one of the three can — or should — be eliminated. The first paradigm, then, is germane to the perspective of traditional political philosophy (as, perhaps we should add, conceived and practised in western culture). Its most famous representative texts are Plato's *Republic*, Rousseau's *Social Contract*, Hegel's *Philosophy of Right*, T.H. Green's *Lectures on the Principles of Political Obligation*, and Oakeshott's *On Human Conduct*. The gist of the message to be found in these (and many other) philosophical texts is that the state is essentially moral community or moral association, possessing proper moral authority, and meting out impartial justice. The language connoted here, not surprisingly, is also that to be found in the discourse of the political marketplace, i.e. in the statesman's or politician's rhetoric; closely related as it is to the traditional perspectives of jurisprudence and theology, this language is the one preferred by the state itself; it is where the state (namely individuals acting within and for the state) is most comfortably at home.

What is being termed here the literary paradigm is the direct opposite of the preceding one. It represents the individual point of view, reflecting the situation of the single (and to some extent) isolated human being, the citizen or subject, faced with the impersonality of society, the indifference of his/her fellow human beings, and as it may be the actual hostility of the state. The image of the state now is not that of a cosy moral community but naked force, something alien, menacing and unknowable outside. This is, assuredly, very far from being the state's own language; not to be found in political rhetoric, it arises out of spontaneous feelings and instinctive reactions, a language which barely rises to the customary academic level. We do find it, quite often, in philosophy, though scarcely in political philosophy. In a way, St Augustine's *City of God* partakes of the paradigm, and so do with differing degrees of explicitness the philosophical texts of Stirner, Tucker, Kierkegaard and the latter-day existentialists. But the realm where this paradigm finds its true home is undoubtedly fictional literature, with its — in our western culture at any rate — high and exclusive tendency to individuate. The main character is necessarily, and almost by definition, alone, both in trouble with and at the same time troubling, society outside. The ways in which literature develops the theme are of course extremely varied and it is only in a loose, evocative sense that we can be permitted to talk about a paradigm. Yet the theme and the direction exist and they do express something very important about society, politics and the state; a language that we look for in vain in either political philosophy or social science. Representative examples might be *Antigone, Hamlet, Caleb Williams, Tess of the d'Urbervilles, Crime and Punishment, Good Soldier Svejk, Keep the Aspidistra Flying, 1984, The Castle*, and *The Lost Honour of Katharina Blum* — another score of titles could be added by anybody to this list without great effort.

The third vocabulary of the state we shall be identifying in this paper falls, as it were, between the two extremes of moralistic–legalistic universalism and atomistic–antinomian individualism. Here, we might say, we enter for the first time into the realm of academic discussion proper; of course the language connoted is not just hovering forlornly in the middle between philosophy and literature but can in a valid and relevant sense (though not in the very strong sense sometimes claimed for it by social science imperialists) be said to be their higher unity or synthesis. For this paradigm and in this language the state ceases to be either warm intimacy or cold externality; here we rise above metaphysics and rhetoric and we leave aside spontaneity and emotion; the intention is analytical, the language is precise, measured, deadpan. Indeed, as opposed to the literary and philosophical paradigms, here it is rather difficult — if not impossible — to find ready-made and recognizable equivalents, conversational partners from the wide world outside. The language of social science caters for social science, nothing else. Through this gaze the state, then, assumes the shape of a visible, perfectly intelligible, transparent entity, an object which is treated with polite interest, rather than reverence or loathing. It is an institution with a wide and complicated surface but without any depth; political culture or ideology (depending on which valuational position the social scientist adopts in carrying out his investigations), i.e. the state's *own* language as well as the spontaneous language of individuals, comes after structure, after objective processes and relationships. What is important about the state is that it is a repository of power, that it is an institution whose chief, or perhaps sole, function is to deal with conflict, with the adjustment of diverse interests arising out of society. The social science paradigm comprises language-users both on the Right and on the Left, though probably it has more affinity, certainly in modern times, with political radicalism than with conservatism (as the philosophical language of the state is more easily allied with an overall conservative perspective). Again, we find for this paradigm a long and respectable historical pedigree, from sections of Aristotle's *Politics* and Machiavelli's *Prince* to the venerable texts of Ferguson, Marx, Weber, Pareto, Michels, Parsons, Dahrendorf and a host of others.

Here, then, we have these three essential languages of the state presented in a nutshell. There is a picture of the state as heaven, one that tends to describe it as hell, and finally a mundane, earthly approach. All the three, however, are equally capable of being cast in the form of rational arguments, with steps logically following on from one another. Our next task is to flesh out — in a way which, alas, cannot go beyond the bare rudiments — the essential *rationale*, or logic, of the three paradigms, in the same sequence as they were preliminarily presented above. It *is* their natural sequence, to be sure. And therefore in each case we shall endeavour to take the argument to its logical extreme, to the point where a seemingly rational vocabulary reveals itself as being self-contradictory.

To begin with our first paradigm. Obviously the view that the state is moral community rests on a view of morality itself, or on what is to be considered right and wrong conduct. In the mainstream of western culture there runs through a conception of right conduct which, almost, logically implies the moral approach to the state referred to above. You find it in the Mosaic Law, in the Gospels, and in the practical reason of Immanuel Kant. On the formal side this conception of morality specifies a moral law which is eternal, universal, categorical, unconditionally binding, having proceeded from Nature, a divine law-giver, or from our own transcendental reason. The universal moral law, most importantly, ties every rational creature equally: human beings are fundamentally equal in their capacity as moral agents. On the substantive side the view under consideration (and here we are surely entitled to include more than just the mainstream of European culture) specifies certain moral ends which elevate human life — indeed, life in general — as being supremely valuable: moral agents 'ought' not to take life (unless exceptionaly justified) and ought not to inflict harm on one another. The famous Kantian dictum expresses the view most succinctly: treat all human individuals as ends in themselves. Of course it is not argued here that this basic conception of morality is either perfectly coherent or all-inclusive or uniformly held by all our revered sages — or, for that matter, that western moral agents have stood out in history with their exemplary observance of these, and derived, categorical imperatives. That is not the point. What *is* important is to recognize in this view the philosophical basis of the paradigm of the state which defines the state as essentially moral community.

We move then on to society. Moral agents do and must live together. How can they do this? Through engaging in practices (for example production, enterprise, art, education, marriage and family) which presuppose the acceptance of common rules of conduct. The universal moral law is abstract: it is transmitted through a variety of customs, religious and cultural traditions, historically evolving identities and personal relationships. The diversity of traditions is enormous but not infinite: certain practices, like slavery or the burning of widows, do not fit (or at any rate not very easily). The view of the state then emerges which defines the association as the concrete legal, governmental and jurisdictional expression of diverse traditions which themselves stand on the basis of equal moral agency as declared by the universal moral law. The morality of the association proceeds directly from the morality of individuals; it is their good, moral will which, in the aggregate or more precisely as synthesized into a conception of the common good, constitutes the state. It is thus that the law of the state, its fundamental rules defining acceptable and unacceptable conduct in a multiplicity of pursuits and relations, itself becomes *the* moral law, or a direct emanation of it, which members of the association are enjoined to obey unconditionally — after all, what they observe is ultimately their own will, their own reason.

The customary philosophical vocabulary of the state acquires its meaning in this kind of framework. Words like authority, obligation, justice, rights and citizenship now make sense. The authority of the state expresses its moral superiority or at least priority, and obligation is the reverse side of authority. Citizens are constituents of the state, with their specified rights and duties. The state itself is obliged — formally — to acknowledge the equality of moral agency and to mete out justice equally, or equitably, with reference solely to impersonal rules. The law is no respecter of persons. The state, as proceeding directly from individual (and formally equal) moral agency, is above and as such unconcerned with personal fortunes and particular social inequalities. There is, usually, a constitution or basic law which separates the state, as ultimate life-giving substance, from governments of the day and temporary majorities; citizens do have rights against the government (though not against the law itself). There is also at least a *tendency* towards what in modern times is called democratic legislation and government, or the republican form of state: equal moral agency and legal equality do create an atmosphere favourable to the acceptance of formal political equality, majoritarianism, even a measure of social equalization (for example welfare legislation), as long as this is seen compatible with the will of the community and its traditional ethos. Lastly but most significantly the state has power, a concentration of physical and instrumental force, and/or psychological and cultural influence, which is legitimately employed to protect the state against external and internal enemies. Citizens have a right to equal protection by the power of the state, and this is as it were purchased by their acceptance of legal, moral and political obligation. Power, of course, is not just the aggregate of various forces but is miraculously transformed into a moral agency when operative on the state level; power, too, like everything else in the state, proceeds from authority which in turn proceeds from the universally binding, eternal moral law.

But can power be adequately explained and comprehended in these terms alone? Political philosophers have always had difficulties here. Somehow, the state as externally observed has never quite managed to match its internal, conceptual identity; the moral being of the state is not quite the same as its empirical being. Is this just an historical accident, capable of solution in principle? Let us see. It could be argued that the discrepancy does actually follow from the morality of the state itself, implied in the very notion of legitimate state power as the supposed emanation of authority and ultimately the moral will of individuals. We can see this quite easily if we concentrate on what's going on at the edges of the moral life of the state. Two institutions, ubiquitously present and in appearance perfectly harmonious with universal moral principles, deserve particular attention here. One is law-enforcement. The law, obviously, has to be enforced; this, after all, is what legitimate state power is *for*. But what does law-enforcement really mean? It means that when power is actually used, it no longer reflects the morality of the law (and hence of the state) directly but rather in an inverted manner, as its practical contradiction. Enforcement signifies that the law, in each particular case, is no longer happily, freely, naturally accepted by the citizen. The state postulates equality of moral agency; yet law-enforcement elevates a *particular* agency with superior rights and duties, an agency which symbolizes (and embodies) the universality of the state in a special way. All citizens of the state are moral constituents of the state and the state proceeds from their will; yet in law-enforcement the citizen is — and must be — treated *as though* he or she were an outsider, an alien, a potential enemy, an external object.

The second state institution, namely punishment, reveals the discrepancy even more dramatically. Every state, without exception, maintains the absolute right to inflict punishment, in accordance with the law, on its individual citizens. Now punishment need not mean harshness, cruelty, draconian judicial sentences, the maltreatment of offenders or even the prominence of the principle of retribution. Whether punishment is harsh or mild, justified on grounds of deterrence or remedial impact, in all cases it means a *clash* of actual wills, a direct confrontation of the moral community and the individual. Otherwise it would make no sense at all, even in the perspective of the most benign of political philosophers. It has often enough been argued that in taking on just punishment the offender himself wills his own execution, incarceration, fining or whatever the case may be. This, indeed, happens sometimes. But while the free, conscious, moral acceptance of punishment is psychologically dubious in the general case, the point is that it is also logically otiose for punishment to be legitimate. You may accept punishment willingly but you need not. Your deep, concealed, ultimate moral will is not important here at all. What is absolutely necessary for punishment to work in practice (and to make sense in theory) is that your present, actual, conscious intention and interest be pitted against the might and right of the state and be overwhelmed by it. If in this sense punishment were not directed *against* the individual, it would not deter, there would be nothing for it to reform and even less would it be proper moral retribution. Individual or majority consent may be required, in civilized, constitutional states, for laws in general. Consent is not required for punishment in the individual case by the individual concerned. This consent is not only irrelevant but, as we have said, contradictory and counterproductive. Nothing, and least of all your own individual desires, will, feelings, principles, exempt you from the law. This is so in the US and in the USSR and no less in the UK. Being a Stuart Legitimist or anarchist or Irish Republican, and refusing to recognize the legitimacy of a court of law in the UK, leaves you exactly where you were before: subject to the law and amenable to punishment. Tell the judge, a ridiculous old fogey dressed in theatrical garb, to bugger off and leave you alone; you see where you will end up.

This mildly irreverent language is designed to introduce us to the second large and essential paradigm of the state, which takes off at this point. It highlights the nature of the state from a radically different, indeed diametrically opposed angle, that of the single individual subject of the state. The state as moral community, as we have seen, already implicitly postulates its own opposite, through its fringe activities, appearing as power directly, and as morality only indirectly. To put it in another way, the good and universal moral will of human beings, producing the state as it were out of itself, already has implicit reference to *another* kind of identity, another layer or manifestation of human willing. We might want to call this second identity here the natural will or identity of individuals. This natural will is undoubtedly *there*, not only discoverable through a logical analysis of the moral perspective of the state but also as a datum of immediate individual consciousness and experience. We do not, that is to say, normally, regularly or emphatically identify with the state, or with organized society around us in general, in our individual aspirations and activities. If anything, we do tend to relate to the state externally, enduring its presence passively or, which is the more interesting case, experiencing it as *constraint*, hemming us in with its myriad rules and regulations. The definition of the state as moral community, we tend to feel, is just an edifying fairy-tale for children; the reality is vastly different. The Dunkirk spirit is an exception and meant to be an exception; the normal condition of the citizen is that of one-sided subjection, indifference, mild or severe alienation. Now this radical individual position *vis-à-vis* the state, though rarely rising to the level of a fully-fledged paradigm, nevertheless has its own distinctive language, supplying the framework for a rich vocabulary which (typically) contains such words as freedom, oppression, suppression, solitude, distance, exposure, fear, resistance, incomprehension and revolt. The point is that the position here referred to is not really contingent: we are *all* in it some of the time, and some people most of the time, and the confrontation, which reflects the inadequacy of the state to its supposed moral ideal, is experienced by all in varying degrees of intensity. A few considerations will show this.

In the first place, it is not strictly speaking true that the power of the state adequately protects individuals against internal and external threats. Punishment, as deterrence or as retribution, protects the citizen only, as abstract moral agency, although the general obviously coincides with the concrete particular — but in a general way only. From my unique individual point of view (and after all I only have this *one* life, this one health, this one security of limb and life-conditions) it is this very coincidence which is contingent. It is a fat consolation for me to know that my murder might be revenged by the law or that other would-be murderers will be deterred or reformed; no compensation will completely eradicate the suffering caused by the actions or negligence of forces outside my control, human agencies supposedly under the authority and power of the state. My effective protection is determined to a large extent by pure chance. For all the might of the state, anybody can be a victim and being a victim means suffering a minus — a consciousness of radical insecurity and isolation — which the plus of retrospective state action can never bring into balance. The state thus reveals itself in the first instance as being too weak, too ramshackle, too distant to justify itself as moral community, as my true 'home'.

But, going a step further, by the same token the state is also, well-nigh invariably, too strong for my liking as an individual. Just as effective protection depends largely on chance, so do my overall life-plan, my own conscious intentions and actions depend for their successful pursuit to a great, maybe unduly great, extent on my individual situation *vis-à-vis* people around me, including appointed representatives of the state. The universal moral law is mediated through the traditions of my society and the laws of my state; but these are further mediated through my own relationship to the concrete manifestations of law, custom, culture. My abstract rights are clearly not enough; in every case I need to be understood and helped (or at least not positively hampered) by my neighbour, by witnesses to a crime or accident, by the patrolling policeman, the solicitor, my local MP or councillor, by the ombudsman, by my boss or shop-steward, by the clerk behind the dole-counter. And what if I get directly in trouble with the law? How is punishment actually experienced by me? Here we have to write in boldly what was only obliquely indicated in our earlier reference to the institution of punishment, then considered in the context of the philosophical paradigm. To the individual punishment is also a *minus*, whether deserved or not. Punishment is measured out to correspond to the supposed magnitude of a specific action (or series of actions), and it in principle excludes all considerations of background, past, present and future. But I experience punishment *not* as a performer of particular actions but as a whole person, a single individual who counts for the state as a unit and a case comparable to others but who counts for himself as, essentially, his whole substantive world.

There is at least a residual — but from the individual point of view all-important — sense in which all rules, all laws, however benign and reasonable, come from the 'outside'. Individual consent might be given but its consequences can never be fully foreseen or rationally predicted. Individuals cannot, as Hobbes would have it, irrevocably authorize the sovereign state to act on their behalf and bind future generations. Individuals are not really capable, let alone spontaneously willing, such a thing, of totally alienating themselves to the community, as in Rousseau's well-known dictum. Such idealism is clearly contradicted by ordinary experience and commonsense. And note that hitherto we considered the state — through the prism of individual consciousness — as being *really* what it is in principle, namely moral association predicated on equal moral agency, impartial justice, formally free and equal access to the law and government. Even in this ideal, heavenly scenario, there is a degree of irreducible externality. But as we very well know, in practice states do not operate like that. The in-built tendency towards constitutionalism and equal involvement of the citizenry in affairs of state is severely checked in most cases. Practical, and even formal, authorization of state action by the citizen body does not go very far. In a liberal-democratic state citizens are normally authorized to elect representatives and certain limited sections of government personnel; they don't, as a rule, vote on administration personnel, on basic economic structure, on the bosses, on the armed forces, on war and peace, certainly not on the law itself. In the USSR the individual citizen is not expected to judge whether or not the Communist Party of the Soviet Union is really the 'leading element' in society. And what happens if you are in a minority, even though taking an equal part in decision-making? In a minority of one perhaps? Your citizenly duties go on regardless. One could easily continue on this level, listing other discrepancies in the moral nature of the state, as approached from the individual point of view.

But we can go even deeper than this. Rules governing conduct within and for the state contain an important element of externality and therefore, to that extent at least, they constrain individuals. There is, however, something constraining in the very *idea* of rule itself, in analytical separation from state, law, society, and *par excellence* in the idea of a moral rule. We have to confront now the basic moral conception, prefacing the moral approach to the state, head-on. It may be universal morality (à la Moses, Zeno, St Paul and Kant) that ultimately defines us as human beings proper. We may — probably do — have something like an elemental moral self or good will. But at the same time morality itself *constrains*, and it must do, otherwise it would not enter into consciousness in the form of binding, general rules at all. Morality, at the very minimum, postulates consistency, discontinuity, arbitrariness, sharp breaks in the pattern. If morality is goodness, the sanctity of life, then it excludes wickedness, the disvaluing of life, one's own and those of others. If morality is reason, then it has not to do with natural instinct and emotion. If it involves the rational planning of one's life, then it must go against spontaneity. Morality connoting peace, civility, decency cannot encounter war, rudeness, violence, malevolence. If morality postulates equal human moral agency, then it necessarily contradicts my uniqueness as a concrete individual. Now what we are suggesting here — and it is not as absurd as it might sound at first — is that these natural elements in the make-up of individual consciousness do play an important part in the way in which the state is perceived and understood from below. As we, minimally perhaps but nonetheless, partake of the tragedy of Antigone, the suffering of Tess and Caleb Williams, the bewilderment of K the Land Surveyor, so we also have a bit of the cock-a-snooping Svejk in us, not to mention the murderous Raskolnikov. The Old Adam is alive and kicking — as well as being kicked. 'L'homme revolté' coexists with 'der pflichtmässige Staatsbürger'.

But now let us think a bit more seriously about the perspective on the state just portrayed. It is real enough, without the slightest doubt, as a common emotional condition and even as 'language', impassioned but coherent within its own terms. Yet similarly to the edifying fairytale we heard earlier, this gothic tragicomedy will also be found wanting on closer analysis, revealed as ultimately self-contradictory and thus fit to be superseded by a more satisfactory, rounded point of view. The figure of the lonely, suffering, rebellious, rule-defying, natural individual confronting the state is really quite *empty* and wholly *negative*. It is, if you like, pure, amorphous energy, Mephistophelian resistance, a substratum of consciousness, perhaps the most important source of creative art and literature, the stuff of mysticism. As such, however, it is politically as well as academically irrelevant. The pure individual merely grumbles about the state and about moral rules; he cannot effectively oppose it, relate to it, or even understand it properly from this position of absolute negativity. If the state is approached totally from the outside, it means that literally *nothing* can be brought up to fill this negative approach with positive content. Total individual freedom, total anomie, is meaningless, and so is total suppression or alienation. Absolute negation, the great refusal, resistance to rules as such, wallowing in antinomian posturings, provides no *alternative* to the prevailing state of affairs. Thus this stance at the end reveals itself as the very opposite of what it appeared at first. Revolt slides into passivity, into indifference. And finally, if all rules, all concrete identities and relationships are found constraining, then in the last resort there is no justification (intellectual or emotional) left to oppose *this* particular set of rules, this government and this socioeconomic system. The prevailing turns out to be as good as any other. Grumbling, indeed, presupposes and positively demands the continuing existence of its target. The state, then, on this level and in terms of this paradigm is ultimately accepted *in toto*. The vocabulary of absolute individualism is rousing, inspirational, but it says nothing of real interest about the nature of the state; it has no conception of conflict, of the clashing of interests, of the extent and limits of power.

It is important to grasp the intellectual inadequacy of this language of the state (its practical impotence is not really of great concern here), in order to understand the emergence and *rationale* of the paradigm which we are associating with social science. We shall make an effort, therefore, actually to derive the language of social science from the language of literature — which, needless to say, is not how the former is usually presented in the texts. The departure is already provided in the idea of individual uniqueness. Now, as we have said, uniqueness is definitely real, an essential aspect of consciousness looked at *internally*, subjectively; for myself I am certainly unique. But this is not the case viewed externally. Not only are other people in society not unique to me but I am not unique myself, in my relation to other people and as I actually experience and comprehend this relationship myself. In our social being we all bear *particular* identities, a multiplicity of overlapping (and sometimes conflicting) *roles*, which make us universally substitutable, and indeed makes social relations possible in the first place. In social practice the two layers or aspects of identity cannot be divorced: *who* I am is inextricably tied to *what* I am. Now there is an infinite number of these particular identities, not to mention their permutations, and obviously most of them are negligible when it comes to understanding organized society and the state, and arrive at a point of view which is more satisfactory than the two essential paradigms so far considered. That I am a flatfooted animal fetishist and collector of old beer mats is of little interest to the student of the state, since — and this is the crucial point — these particular identities are also of little interest to *me* in my relationship to the state.

But then, equally obviously, some particular identities *do* count in this respect. To use the example of punishment again, my unique suffering in, say, being sentenced to a term of imprisonment puts me at the same time into the particular social category of defendant and afterwards I become a part of the prison population, sharply distinguished from the rest of society, both in fact and in consciousness. Whether I like it or not, and whether or not I have a positive desire emotionally to identify with my fellow prison inmates, I will have at least some *interest* shared with them, for example in petitioning for better quality food, more exercise, etc. But perhaps even this example is somewhat contrived and fails to carry enough conviction, since — thankfully — prison experience is both temporary and confined to a small minority of the population in settled states. There are, however, particular identities which are enduring (even if not lifelong), which embrace the whole of personality (as beer mat collection probably doesn't) and which have sociopolitical import. Such identities include, most significantly, wealth, status, ethnicity, education, age and gender — not necessarily in this order of priority. Being male or female, poor or rich, living on the dole or off the profit on my gilt-edged shares, a teenager or a menopausal widow, an Oxford graduate with a home counties accent or a West Indian speaking patois, are identities which count for me, individually, but which at the same time define my most important relationships to other people and to the state. There is a correlation here between subjective identity and sociopolitical position, and here we also see how these identities — social positions — connect up with *power*. At the least what we become aware of at this point is that people, on account of their particular social position (and not on account of their subjective individuality), are *differentially* related to the state, a supposedly universal entity comprising equal moral agents. The social science paradigm of the state is based on this fundamental recognition.

Here, on the level of science, the state is approached dispassionately, looked at sideways, not from deep within (as in traditional philosophy) and neither from beneath, cringing or grumbling. The state is observed: what does it look like? It will appear now, in its fundamental contours, as a definite structure, a network of interlocking offices and institutions, accompanied by a given set of cultures, i.e. beliefs, ideologies, patterns of conscious behaviour. In the characteristic language of social science, though in considerably varying degrees of course, the latter element is usually played down. Structures and processes (i.e. structures changing in a more or less regular manner) come first, ideas — justifications and accusations — come second. The state is primarily objective, it is a fact. What is the chief distinguishing mark of this fact? It is the concern with power. Any given state is to be seen and described as the visible expression of a *power-settlement*, the outcome of a struggle among various forces and factors in society, chiefly to do with the position and interest of particular groups (which we introduced above as particular identities) and individuals as the bearers of social roles. In other words, the state reflects a given, prevailing pattern of the societal distribution of power. It may, more or less, be an autonomous structure, and not just a negative reflection of power-relations within society, but the concentrated power it embodies nevertheless has to do with *social* positions. What else would the state be concerned with? Politics, as the activity of minding the state, is to be understood, in the well-known definition of an American social scientist, in terms of who gets what, when, how. It follows, then, that social science looks at the state as an historically and geographically *specific* entity, without a common deeper essence; states are comparable only to the extent of displaying this external characteristic of the concern with power. Ethical relativism (in approaching the state, that is, not generally) usually underlines this language: the state may be 'good' or otherwise, meting out 'justice' or otherwise, but this has little or nothing to do with it being a state, properly so-called. It is a state if it has 'majesty', if it successfully maintains and wields power within and over society. So we see in St Augustine, in Bodin, in Max Weber.

The vocabulary of the state in the paradigmatic language of social science contains such key-words as conflict, interest, adjustment and effectiveness (as well, of course, as a host of others, relating to the functions of state offices in policy formulation and administration). Conflict explains the origin, existence and nature of the state; if there were no conflicts in society, states would not have arisen or be needed now. Conflict, of course, does not mean war; the state, after all, embodies *peace*, it stands for settlement, regularity, orderly processes. But peace through the state does not signify anything like natural harmony among groups and role-bearers in society. It means that groups accept, willy-nilly as the case may be, the practical necessity of co-operation, as having at least short-term advantages. But for any group or role-bearer the prevailing settlement is either precarious or means a second-best among theoretically conceivable scenarios or indeed just bearable. Groups are ranked according to their access to, and share of, the concentrated power of the state. The position of one group is gained at the expense of others who therefore have to be constantly watched. And the latter similarly keep an eye on possible openings for the improvement of their own power-position. Citizens of the state acting as group-members and role-bearers follow what they conceive as their interest within the prevailing situation; it may be either maintaining the present structure, with possibly the erection of further safeguards, or radically altering it. Politics is a competitive game and the state represents the temporary result of race-meetings. Certain conventions grow up, themselves originating in group conflict. These have the function of adjusting competitive and conflicting interests, and they can do this more or less effectively. Government works if social conflict is reduced to disagreements about policy, about the means and not the end. A state is ungovernable if its customary processes of interest adjustment prove inadequate and the disaffection of certain, potentially powerful, groups call the game itself into question. Then another game, with different rules and reflecting a new configuration of social power, might be started. But in all cases justice follows from the legitimacy (i.e. broad acceptance) of the prevailing state-form, and that in turn follows from the actual power of groups in pursuing their interest.

This is obviously a simplified account of a very complex picture presented by the social science approach which in reality has a much more extensive and intricate vocabulary. But hopefully it is not a distorted account. We have, of course, abstracted from the language of social science words which properly belong to the other two languages, in order, mainly, to show its coherence, its supposed conceptual independence. Claims to this independence and coherence have, of course, been made from time to time. Perhaps the most conspicuous and extreme examples are furnished by, on the one side, what is sometimes called vulgar marxism, and on the other side the end of ideology phase of western 'empirical science'. For the former the state has no other essence apart from its role in maintaining the power of the ruling class over oppressed classes. For the latter the essence of the state is the maintenance of an acceptable social equilibrium where all important interests find a niche, i.e. access to decision-making. Here we might make the explicit point, already referred to in passing, that the supposed ethical relativism, or value-neutrality, accompanying the social science approach, is and *has to be* confined to the actual object of investigation, namely the state as it appears to the scientific investigator. No social scientist has ever been value-neutral and there has never been a significant and substantial scientific account of the state which would not, *objectively*, have favoured one or another value-position. Broadly speaking, they would go either in a radical direction, i.e. implicitly pointing towards a feasible alternative to the existing set-up, or in a conservative direction, i.e. conflating and identifying the ideal (the alternative) with the actually existing. But this consideration by itself does not necessarily invalidate the method or language of social science: it *is* possible, *within* the given overall framework, to couch explanations of the state which are more or less accurate, consistent, helpful in detailed social science research.

What, it may be argued, is common to social science paradigms of both Left and Right is the claim to *transparency*. Social science, the language of interest, conflict and power, lays bare the real nature of the state, as the other two languages fail to do. It is the last word, the highest, most satisfactory approach to the subject. The language of morality as well as the language of individual experience can be relegated to the background; they have become otiose. After the edifying fairy-tale and the horrifying romance now we are in the possession of a sex-manual which really tells us what's what. Now it is not to be denied that in a profound and relevant sense the language of social science *is* more advanced, more satisfactory, more rounded and more fertile than the other two we have considered. It is not only more extensive and internally varied but has the feature of logical elegance, neatness, clarity, and an undoubted force of intellectual conviction. Historically and in very broad terms, we might say, it is this language which has emerged victorious, thus proving its worth. The paradigm of political philosophy is that which dominates the classical period of western civilization: Greece and Rome. Medieval Christianity represents the sway and ascendancy of the 'individualist' point of view (in the sense of individual destiny 'transcending' the state in the present Valley of Tears). In the modern age, from Renaissance and Reformation onwards but particularly from the second half of the nineteenth century, we have been witnessing the triumphant march of a growing science of society. It is this language alone that we tend to take really seriously, in sane and sober moments when we want clarification and enlightenment, rather than thrills and uplifting. The language of social science, it appears, has even managed to synthesize and incorporate what was relevant to proper understanding in the other two paradigms, while leaving the student of the state free to continue to enjoy literature and maybe also to engage in a bit of harmless philosophical speculation. It is truly extremely difficult, even in abstract terms, to envisage ways in which the language of social science itself could be transcended, creating a wholly novel idiom of understanding.

But this is not quite the end of the story. While it may prove impossible to move forward from social science, it does make a difference how we judge the nature of the social science synthesis. It is possible to adopt two positions. One is what was referred to earlier in passing as social science imperialism: here the view taken is that the other two vocabularies of the state have been *superseded* in a really substantial and irrevocable way; either they are subsumable under the umbrella of social science or they are sheer pastime. The other position — very resolutely taken in this paper — is one of (for want of a more expressive term) social science tolerance. This means the recognition that the other two languages are also, within certain limits, independent and indispensable for a proper understanding, co-ordinated with and not subordinate to social science; as they have their limits, so does social science. In the first place, an approach of tolerance seems vindicated in the light of actual evidence and experience in the living world of states. Social science imperialism is conspicuous for its failure; the state, if anything, has remained just as opaque as it ever was. The two lesser languages keep reappearing in ostensibly very different contexts, in new surroundings. The resemblance of newly created states, following on revolutionary resettlements, to the state of old is too close for comfort. Similarly the onset of economic prosperity and the politics of consensus has not made any appreciable difference to rhetoric heard in the political marketplace. In the west there is no end of ideology and in the east there is no withering away of the state, either in practice or in theory. All states still, be they advanced socialist or advanced industrial, are accounted for in universal terms as moral associations, in the language of Plato, Rousseau and Hegel. They enshrine the formal equality of citizens as moral agents, specify legal rights, sanction constitutional processes, mete out impartial justice. The symbolic paraphernalia of the state as moral community are in evidence everywhere: flags, emblems, the aura of authority, the claims on unquestioning loyalty and obligation. And correspondingly the language of antinomian revolt and resistance, of alienation, isolation, despair, of poetic individual transcendence, flows on unabating. There is no end to the discrepancies in the identity of the state, to its mystery and ambiguity, to its incomprehension in terms of anything less than a plural perspective.

It is only fair to say that in past decades there has been a salutary ebbing in the imperialistic thrust of social science language-users, clearly recognizing the limits of their clarificatory endeavours. In the west we have seen the rebirth of political philosophy, the reappearance of accredited problems of authority, obligation, equality and the like — all of which merely signifies the acceptance, granted grudgingly at first, of the autonomy of political philosophy, of its being something more than a humble handmaiden to social science (which it was regarded as, in the heyday of Weldonesque compilations of vocabularies). And marxism these days is anything but vulgar. It is rich, sophisticated, discerning, internally varied but at the same time clearly in danger of losing its erstwhile robust message, namely that the state is the organ of class-rule, pure and simple. The state now has relative autonomy (as in Poulantzas), its mainstay is cultural hegemony, not sheer power (as in Gramsci), ideological discourse is to co-exist with the marxist science of historical formations even after the overthrow of capitalism (as in Althusser). Where do we go from here?

In this paper we shall conclude by briefly — and no doubt inadequately — indicating why there might be good intellectual reasons, as distinguished from the evidence of observation, for believing that the three essential languages will persist for some time to come, and that they are perhaps best seen as complementary, mutually reinforcing, rather than being locked in murderous competition. There are two points to be made, epitomized respectively in these two pithy sentences of Biblical derivation: 'I am not always my brother's keeper' and 'we don't live by bread alone.' The first epitome is meant to supply the rationale of what we have been calling the vocabulary of antinomian individualism, as exemplified in the idiom of creative literature. How could this language, this experience of living in the state, be possibly overcome and eliminated? This could only be done if we were to maintain that the relationship of the single individual to the state is radically, dimensionally different from other, lesser, more intimate group-relationships; that the experienced alienation of the individual in and from the state, and the laws and power of the state constraining the individual, had simply and solely to do with such things as the *size* of the state, its being remote and aloof from the individual, its *specific* structure. In other words, it would have to be maintained that otherwise, and as it were naturally, I *am* my brother's keeper, that is, that there is nothing fundamentally alienating, oppressive, constraining, resistance-provoking, in human group-relations *as such*. Is there any telling reason to believe that this is so? There are lots of reasons: introspective, experiential, observational, historical, anthropological, for believing that it is *not* so. Individual consciousness *is* individual consciousness, and my life-experience is my life-experience uniquely, unrepeatably. There is a subjective, inner, if you like, infinite, dimension to me that my external relationships cannot match and cannot fill. There is a gap, however tiny, between my closest group and myself, and from this it follows that *all* my external relationships are subject, in principle, to the rather disturbing experiences of loneliness, suppression, estrangement, the consciousness of being hemmed in and wanting to break out. Where the individual–state situation differs from others is in quantity, rather than quality. The implication of this is surely that supposed radical alternatives to the existing state will not very much affect or alter this situation — which is not to say, of course, that given reforms, even revolutions, could not be very significant in terms of the improvement of the particular power-positions of certain groups and social role-bearers (*not* individuals). Whatever society and state we live under, as the highly discerning marxist author, Ernst Fischer, once wrote, there is always a 'necessity of art'. To which one may perhaps be allowed to add: including the necessity of the *art of the state*.

But if, assuming that the paragraph above contained any rational sense, the literary language of the state is vindicated, then we can find equally convincing arguments to show that the philosophical — or 'moral' — vocabulary of the state is also basically valid, to be upheld and given proper appreciation. 'We do not live by bread alone', i.e. it is definitely *not* the case that interest and power supply adequate explanatory principles for an understanding of the state. It is not true, in the first place, that individual political actors in their capacity of concrete role-bearers just simply promote their group interest. Interest is abstract and meaningless in the absence of a consideration (semi-conscious maybe) of *propriety*. Capitalists and workers, native white Anglo-Saxons and Asian immigrants, pursue their interests guided by what they believe is right; their particular position, in other words, is approximated to, really inseparable from, a dimly perceived *universal* position, to be expressed in terms of general laws, in the provision of impartial justice to be meted out to equal moral agents. Of course there is conflict about what the correct definition of propriety or justice is but the point remains that it is universality that is sought by the conflicting parties and that this sought-after universality answers the general moral definition of the state. Where separate and conflicting groups can co-exist side by side is *the* state, by definition. Interest presupposes morality, particular adjustments presuppose universal justice.

It is the same with power. The power wielded by the state does not come from nature, it is not the superior (physical or mental) strength of individuals. Force is not just aggregated, added up, to yield power: it is the synthetic outward expression of *unity* as consciously willed and maintained by people making up the state. This unity must come first, and power is only its outward, secondary consequence, and we might indeed want to say that it is this *will* towards unity, this human tendency to conceive of a common good, to work for it, to make sacrifices for it, to defend it by force, which comes ultimately from nature, so ubiquitous and so enduring is the evidence of the state. And the will towards unity is of course the same thing as the moral will: it is because human beings tend to conceive of universal rules of right and wrong that they form associations defined in terms of moral authority, it is because the recognition of the moral authority of the state is basic that the association has also an embodiment recognized as power, and finally it is because the state exists as an independent and prior principle that there can be such a thing as the playing out of conflicting group interests and particular role-identities. No morality — no state — no society. But — of course! — again this is not the *end* of the story but its *beginning*: since the language of political philosophy can describe for us only the sublime principle of the state, and cannot properly account for its skewed actual manifestation, its residual hardness and externality (as my heaven is still some distance from me, however strenuously I might try to rise to sublime heights), we shall have, inevitably, recourse to the language of literature, and since this vocabulary in turn fails to fill the basic individual predicament with explanatory content, we shall turn again to the language of social science. And so it goes on.

© 1989 R.N. Berki

Chapter three

Marxism, Democracy and the Public Sphere

Christopher Pierson

Few propositions in contemporary social and political analysis could properly be claimed to be axiomatic. However, it is possible to identify a widespread, if not general, consensus that the past 15 to 20 years have seen both an acute crisis in the political institutions of the advanced capitalist world and matching, at times, even surpassing this, a crisis of confidence in the capacity of the conventional tools of political analysis to diagnose, let alone offer remedies for, this political malaise. This is quite clearly the sense of a number of recent contributions, from John Dunn's *Western Political Theory in the Face of the Future* to André Gorz's *Farewell to the Working Class*. It is a conviction most baldly stated by Andrew Gamble, who insists that 'for the present modern Western thought appears to have reached an impasse'.[1]

For some time, there was a broadly-held belief, 'on the left', that this was, in essence, an impasse confined to 'bourgeois' political science, whose predominantly consensual and pluralistic models of political life were quite unable to explain the widespread upsurge in political and industrial militancy in advanced Western capitalist societies from the late 1960s onwards. But in more recent years, confidence that, in contrast to this exhaustion of 'bourgeois' political science, marxist political discourse was able to offer not only the means of interpreting but also the revolutionary medium for changing both the theory and practice of western political institutions, has ebbed. It is now seen to be much more deeply implicated in the general crisis of Western political theory and, even among those who acknowledge its considerable strengths, both its theoretical and strategic cogency is now much more widely questioned. With the waning of confidence in marxism, the edifice of socialist theory is now, as much as ever, a tower of Babel of competing ideologies and strategies.[2]

It is against this background that, in this paper, I critically examine a number of recent 'post-marxist' initiatives which seek to address the problems of democratic politics, in the light of the perceived weaknesses of traditional marxist explanations, and assess the extent to which these initiatives may be expected to deliver useful theoretical advances.

I begin with a brief summary of the most common generic weaknesses that have been widely identified with 'classical' marxist political analysis:

1 Historicism

Historicism — as confidence in immanent if tendential laws of historical development — is extraordinarily deep-seated in marxist theory. From the neo-Hegelian anticipation of True Democracy as 'the first true unity of the particular and the universal' to the overcoming of the cumulative self-obstruction of productive forces under developed capitalism through the socialization of ownership, the expectation that continued development favours progressive social forces with an interest in socialism is a ubiquitous marxist claim. Marx's own sensitivity to the interdependence of theory and practice and Luxemburg's seemingly open-ended anticipation of either 'socialism or barbarism' notwithstanding, the marxist tradition has been preponderantly committed to the evolutionist expectation that historical development favours progress towards socialism. In certain forms, it has also carried the much more radical claim that historical development, albeit in passing through a period of greatly intensified social struggle, can carry society into circumstances where formal political institutions — the state, political parties, representation, rights' claims and so on — will become obsolete. With hindsight, such evolutionary optimism — best seen in Marx's anticipation of True Democracy as the realization of 'fully human emancipation' — can be seen to be misplaced and even pernicious.

2 The 'Derivation of the Political'

A second pervasive characteristic of marxist analysis has been its tendency to seek to 'derive' political institutions and practices from other aspects of a materialist analysis. This is particularly clear in marxist accounts of the state. Here the point is not to deny the interdependence of state and economy or, more broadly conceived, of state and society but rather to challenge the claim that the nature of this state can be derived from, for example, the 'irreconcilability of class contradictions' or 'the capital form'. For such a claim necessarily entails the subordination of political (and ideological) struggle to economic forms and a sublimation of struggles around differing political axes to struggles based upon class. The consequence of this marxist position seems to be that (all) politics is, in some sense, class politics. Other forms of struggle — over such issues as gender, race and the environment — are allowed some autonomy, but are all seen, in a more or less explicit 'last instance', to be subordinated to the principal

lines of political cleavage defined around social class and the consequences of this attempt to derive all political struggle from class
become still more acute where class is itself characterized in an
acutely derivative form, as in its definition around formal ownership or non-ownership of the means of production. The principal
charge against this marxist determinism is that it denies the very
space in which an authentically non-determined and discursive politics
could arise.

3 Essentialism

A third generic weakness of marxist appraisals of the political has
been seen to lie in the tendency to treat political institutions and practices as *essences* rather than as *capacities*. Here, Leninism has perhaps been the chief offender. In its formulaic insistence that, for
example, every state represents the unmediated rule of a single class
or that democracy necessarily mobilizes the dictatorship of a particular
class, state and democracy are seen to have essential and categorical
qualities. This both draws attention away from the contingent, historical and contestable elements *within* given states and democratic
practices and promotes strategies for socialist transformation which
are themselves essentialist — 'smashing the state', displacement of
'bourgeois democracy' by 'proletarian democracy' and so on. Also
damaging is the widespread marxist conception that the (capitalist)
state necessarily acts in the interests of the ascendant (capitalist) class,
whether in a crudely instrumental sense (as 'the tool of the ruling
class'), or in that more elaborate form which recognizes internal
divisions of the state, but only as the expression of the divided interests
of particular fractions of capital. More damaging still is the expectation that the state, as an expression of the irreconcilable contradictions inscribed in the existence of classes, can be overcome or
'wither away' where these contradictions founded upon class cease to
operate.

4 Holism

A fourth critical weakness of marxist political analysis has been seen
to reside in its thoroughgoing commitment to holistic modes of social
explanation. Here again, the intention is not to deny the very considerable value of such forms of explanation, nor to deny that the
application of marxist methods has often effected a very considerable
advance upon traditional institutional, constitutional and liberal pluralist accounts of the political. But though the reason for marxism's
seeking society-wide or even world-wide explanations is clear, it is

no less evident that not all forms of significant political struggle can best be understood in this context. This is true not only of interstate struggles, which are massively evident but rather poorly explained within conventional marxist analyses, but also of (conceptually) localized disputes within societies — which may not have a national or class-based significance — but which are nonetheless strategic sites of the struggle to secure autonomy. The possibility this raises of socialist pluralism — as anything other than the rather fanciful 'disappearance' of significant political disputes under communism — is very poorly conceptualized by a marxism overwhelmingly committed to holistic patterns of social explanation.

Of course, criticisms of the categorical weaknesses of marxism — its commitment to historicism, derivationism, essentialism, and so on — have long been voiced, perhaps most prominently by Karl Popper and J.L. Talmon, in defence of established liberal democracies and in support of H.B. Mayo's claim that 'Marxist theory . . . is at odds with the democratic use of political action to build the free and just society.'[3] However, in more recent years, many of the same criticisms have been taken up by a range of political theorists who are united less by a shared antipathy to the established marxist political tradition than by a desire critically to appropriate what are seen to be the authentic insights of marxist analysis within an eclectic project, drawing upon several theoretical traditions and directed towards synthesizing a viable, libertarian theory of democratic socialist politics. The central organizing principle of this theoretical reorientation has been an encounter with existing (and unsatisfactory) marxist accounts of the state and of democracy, and the attempt to recast the relations of state and civil society, to take account both of these insufficiencies and of changes in the nature of the state–society relation in contemporary advanced capitalist societies.

Clearly, these more recent accounts have not been conjured out of the air and they show a varying proximity to the major existing strains of socialist (political) discourse. Repeatedly and unsurprisingly, given his sensitivity to the particular difficulties of effecting a socialist strategy within advanced capitalist societies, Gramscian themes are to the fore. This is particularly clear in the work of the later Poulantzas, whose hostility to 'Leninist formalism' was complemented by an emphasis upon the centrality of struggles *within* the state. Hostility to formulaic rubric on the state, recognition of its enabling and emancipatory, as well as its repressive moments, insistence upon the ubiquity of struggles within and about the state, the necessity of state institutions under socialism and a call for the careful study of particular state formations rather than the generic derivation of *the* form of *the* capitalist state, are perhaps the most prominent claims of this initiative. What is also clear, particularly from the work of Claus Offe, is that this is not only a crisis

of the ways in which the state is understood (principally by neo-
marxist theorists) but also a crisis of the state form itself, a crisis of the
welfare state as the characteristic form of the state under social
democracy.

This reassessment of the state has dictated, in its turn, a differing
evaluation of the other term of the state–civil society relation. If
the state was not the undivided and indivisible representative of the
interests of a single class, if it had an emancipatory as well as a
repressive potential and if, above all, it would not and could not 'wither
away' under socialism, it was clear that the traditional marxist understanding of civil society, exhaustively defined by the *bellum omnia
contra omnes* of a market society, would have to be substantially
amended. First and foremost, the belief that political alienation orig-
inates in the division of state and civil society had to be abandoned
and the aspiration to 'overcome' political differences through estab-
lishing the identity of state and civil society vigorously resisted as
both utopian and extremely dangerous. Although the state is regarded
as irreversible, and this not simply as a necessary but wholly undesirable
evil, it is also seen to embody chronic pretensions to exercise ever
greater power and the surest means of holding its powers in check
is seen to lie in a vigorous, independent and legally-guaranteed civil
society.

This independent civil society cannot however be seen to be coter-
minous with the civil society of 'classical' marxist theory. For it is
not a sphere exclusively occupied by classes nor could the forms
of struggle that of necessity traverse it be exclusively defined by
differences of class interest. It is constantly stressed that the basis
of a radical and socialist civil society should be a diversity of struggles
prosecuted by a variety of overlapping but distinct popular groupings
and alliances. At the heart of this advocacy of a reconstituted civil
society lies the substantively unorthodox aspiration for a socialist
pluralism.

In John Keane's *Public Life and Late Capitalism* (1984), this pursuit
of 'a socialist and pluralist civil society' is seen to require the weakening of both public and private bureaucracies in favour of 'the establishment and strengthening of spheres of autonomous public life'.
This entails, in its turn, a reassessment of the 'classical' marxist
understanding of democracy. While this re-evaluation is subject to
a good deal of internal variation, there is a more or less universal
recognition that the marxian aspiration to a 'True' or substantive
democracy is both impossible *and* undesirable and that existing (and
inadequate) democratic practices are something to be retained and
expanded upon wherever possible, rather than to be razed and replaced.
Pluralism, not only of parties but also of ideologies and 'ways of life',
is seen to be an indispensable feature of any satisfactory democratic polity.

For the sake of both clarity and brevity, the most important claims of this recent 'post-marxist' initiative can be summarized as a set of short theses:

On the State:

1 The state does not (either instrumentally or relatively autonomously) function unambiguously in the interests of a single class.
2 The state is not a centralized–unified political actor. It is 'an arena of struggle', constituted–divided by quite opposing interests.
3 There can be no satisfactory, general analysis of the (capitalist) state. The proper subject of study is given nation–states in their historical and international particularity.
4 The state is not an institution that can be 'occupied'; state power is not such that it can be 'seized'. Transformation of the state may be 'profound' but it will also be gradual and, at least in part, internal.
5 The state cannot be overcome and will not wither away; it is essential to any developed society. While not a necessarily evil, it must however always be subject to strict delimitation and control. This may be summarized as a call for the effective restriction of a necessary state power.

On Civil Society and 'Social Pluralism'

6 Any form of socialism which is to realize aspirations for both liberty and equality must be based not upon the overcoming of the division between state and civil society but rather upon their increasingly clear and formalized differentiation.
7 Rather than fostering a socialist morality, civil society must be the site of a legally-guaranteed plurality of aspirations, ways of life and ideologies.
8 Anticipations of 'the end of politics' and the end of conflict over the distribution of means and resources (even under circumstances of abundance) are utopian, as is the corresponding expectation of the overcoming of the necessity of law. Under these circumstances, an (extended) set of civil and political rights, and the state as legal guarantor of these rights, is indispensable.
9 All forms of emancipatory struggle under late capitalism are *not* reducible to forms of class struggle. An emancipatory politics must therefore recognize the significance of new movements (often single-issue campaigns), and recognize the necessity of alliances of liberating forces within a popular-democratic (rather than exclusively class based) struggle.

On Democracy

10 Representative parliamentary democracy and many of the rights and liberties secured under it are real though limited popular achievements.

11 Any attempt to replace all forms of representative democracy by exclusively direct democracy will issue in statism.

'A Socialist and Pluralist Civil Society?'

It is against this background that I want to consider recent attempts to recast democratic socialist theory in terms of the promotion of 'a socialist and pluralist civil society'. This initiative, I would suggest, is generally to be welcomed, particularly in its breach with more orthodox marxist accounts of the state and of the state–civil society relation. However, it is clear that such a general recasting of the realm of non-state institutions is not without its problems. Certainly, some of these can be attributed to the imprecision of terminological usage. Thus, in a number of recent accounts, civil society is understood — rather generally — as being synonymous with society itself or with everything that lies outside the state — and this contrasts with more traditional analyses, particularly those of classical political economy and its critique, in which it is often much more narrowly defined, as referring exclusively to the realm of exchanges within a market economy.[4] But obviously, the differences between competing accounts of civil society are not exhaustively defined by terminological imprecision and here I want to approach some of the more substantive difficulties of recent innovations by considering why more traditional socialist and marxist analyses have tended to be hostile to both 'pluralism' and 'civil society'.

Liberalism and 'Depoliticization'

Generally among socialist commentators, the constitution of a separate civil society is seen to be associated with the *bellum omnia contra omnes* of an emergent market economy, with the reduction of human individuals to acquisitive and predatory egoists constrained only by the rule of law and the reduction of all forms of human interrelation to contractual relations backed by the sanctions of the law. Associative and affective relations are seen to be devalued in a system which gives very substantial means to the wealthy and strong to oppress the poor and the weak. Above all, it does violence to the principle of fraternity. The compelling strength of the specifically marxist account, exhaustively developed in *Capital*, is that civil society defines that realm of authentic though purely formal freedom which is the necessary basis of substantive unfreedom and inequality. The process of free and equal exchange is seen to be the means by which the bourgeoisie expropriates the surplus value of the working class. The relations pertaining within civil society are seen to be systematically exploitative, if not unjust, and to be guaranteed by the untrammelled claims of private property.[5] Thus capitalist society is condemned not simply because it does violence to the values of fraternity and solidarity, nor yet because it promotes vast inequalities of wealth and resources, but, above all, because it denies and conceals the exercise of power that apparently free and equal contractual exchanges necessarily enjoin.

Similar criticisms underpin traditional marxist hostility to pluralism. At its most uncompromising, marxism holds that the advent of socialism precludes pluralism as both unnecessary — given the actual and moral superiority of socialist principles over others — and impossible — given the incompatibility of socialism with the characteristic principles of liberalism and/or capitalism. This 'classical' Marxist position is not premised upon the suppression of a genuine plurality of interests (other than, in the immediate revolutionary period, the interests of the tiny minority of the exploiting bourgeoisie), for it is argued that it is, in fact, possible to establish *objectively* the interests of the several social classes, and that those of the (massively predominant) proletariat accord with the transition to socialism. That sections of the working class should perceive themselves as having an interest in an other than socialist organization of production is attributable to a false and manipulated consciousness, lack of education and 'historical residues' and cannot be seen to be consonant with their *true* interests.

In this form, I should argue, the marxist critique has a very limited purchase on the parameters of liberal pluralism. More telling is that second and less wholesale critique which is directed less against the principle of plurality than against the 'misleading' claims of liberal or liberal–capitalist pluralism. Here, the definitive 'classical' source is Marx's mature critique of political economy. We have seen how the formal plurality of free and equal individuals simultaneously provided the basis for, and a 'masking of', those processes through which capitalism secures substantive inequality and unfreedom. It was the 'freeing' of individuals to pursue unfettered their several interests as the buyers and sellers of commodities (including labour power) that distinguished the inequities of capitalism from its feudal forerunner. In its turn, it is this formal plurality within the capitalist economy which effectively denies substantive pluralism to the great majority of its participants, who find themselves increasingly driven from a variety of modes of life towards a uniformly routinized and meaningless working life under the advanced division of labour.

Similar criticisms have been widely mobilized against much more recent advocates of pluralism. Those like Dahl, Truman and Lipset, who promoted the US of the 1950s and 60s as a model of pluralist democracy, have been subsequently, and deservedly, criticized for presenting an overly-sanguine view of the representation of the a plurality of interests in the US, neglecting or excusing the way in which the American model of pluralism systematically favours big business and other organized corporate interests.[6] Such manifestations, it is argued, are the inevitable result of an advocacy of pluralism that fails to investigate those societal conditions that will always enable formal equality of access and representation to favour particular, and often numerically small, interests.

Recently, more critical pluralists, such as Charles Lindblom, have begun to take much fuller account of the distorting effect of the disproportionate powers of corporate interests upon pluralist political arrangements and this is one source of an apparent convergence of critical pluralist and critical marxist positions. But even this more critical pluralism has found it difficult to resolve the *institutional* problems that such disproportionality poses and certainly the marxist disclosure of the inequity of existing pluralist arrangements is a continuing challenge to any attempt to reconstitute a 'socialist and pluralist civil society'.[7]

Marxism and 'Depoliticization'

At the same time, it is imperative to acknowledge the considerable strengths of liberal accounts in seeking to expose the 'unpolitical' premises of marxist analysis. At first sight, to criticize marxism as 'unpolitical' must, even for its opponents, seem unreasonable, given the former's quite evident and passionate involvement in what can clearly be seen to be political struggles. Yet to politics in its (partial but indispensable) sense, as the processes of practical, discursive will-formation, marxist theory affords comparatively little attention. Again, we can assess this criticism through a brief consideration of marxist positions on civil society and pluralism.

Certainly, marxist writers have been right to question the substantive, as opposed to the purely formal, value of plurality and the 'bourgeois' rights and freedoms of civil society. Yet at least two serious reservations must be entered against this marxist critique. First, it is clear that though limited, these liberties have been of enormous value to popular political movements and that they have exercised an (again limited) constraint upon more directly coercive elements of class rule. (Although, despite the occasional rhetorical flourish, it would be misleading to suggest that marxism has displayed a generalized disregard for 'bourgeois freedoms'.)

A second and potentially more serious reservation focuses upon the conviction that some set of political institutions, albeit not those of liberal parliamentary democracy, are indispensable under *any* envisageable form of societal organization. I have suggested that 'classical' marxian expectations for passing beyond politics were, varying forms of transitional arrangement notwithstanding, wholly unrealistic. I have also argued against the historicist tendency to prescribe 'necessary' political conclusions from given historical developments. If post-revolutionary social arrangements cannot be post-political and if historical development does not determine given political consequences, it becomes clear that space must exist for politics as a sphere for the negotiation of legitimately competing programmes and practices — and this must mean, in its turn, formal political institutions and procedures. Here again some effort has been made, among critical marxists, to reconcile these conclusions with more traditionally marxist premises. But repeated experience suggests that the price of engaging political practice may be a breach with the parameters of 'classical' marxism. For all that it is massively compromised by its identification with concealed structures of inequality and unfreedom, recognition of the necessity of political institutions is a real strength in the liberal critique of marxism.

Similar arguments apply to the marxian appraisal of pluralism. We have seen that this was telling against traditional forms of pluralism which mask systematic inequalities of access to power and decision-making under the formal rubric of equal access to a neutral and adjudicating state. At the same time, in the face of the evidence of forms of oppression not exclusively based upon class and of valued and legitimate differences within the working-class movement, more critical marxists have made significant concessions to less unreservedly apologist defenders of plurality. The consequent diffusion of critical marxist and critical pluralist perspectives has, as McLennan notes, made rigorous opposition of the two less compelling.[8]

Yet there are limitations upon what a marxist perspective can yield to pluralism without thus losing claim to those very criteria that make it distinctively marxist. Instructively, so far as 'classical' marxism, rather than 'actually-existing socialism', is concerned, the real difficulty does not lie, as its opponents so frequently insist, in opposition to pluralism, since we have seen that 'classical' marxism is not, in fact, premised upon the suppression of a genuine plurality of interests. Rather does it rest upon the fact that such anticipations of plurality as one can find in 'classical' marxism lack any *institutional* basis and seem to deny the possibility (under socialism) of the continuation of a *contested* plurality of interests, rather than simply of a 'diversity in abundance'.

Here again then, the radical weakness of 'classical' marxism lies not in its embrace of a drab uniformity but rather in its unrealistic and unpolitical anticipation of diversity secured under circumstances which are almost unimaginably improbable. And again, for all that it is compromised by its association with the legitimation of an inequitable and oppressive social order, liberal recognition of the necessity of institutional plurality must be counted a strength against its 'non-political' marxist opponents.

Public Spheres

One interesting and innovative response to the multiple difficulties presented by the shortcomings of both marxist and liberal, political analysis and uncertainty over the kinds of institutions that should inhabit a reformed civil society, is to be found in the attempt critically to appropriate and restructure the classical liberal principle of *the public sphere*. Here, the definitive source is Jürgen Habermas. Upon his account, the 'classical' public sphere, as the means of mediating relations between society and the state, was characterized by a set of institutions which guaranteed equal access of all citizens to a critical and discursive process in which public authority and political decision-making were to be subject to the rational scrutiny of a 'reasoning public'.[9] In practice, the ascendancy of such discursive public debate, 'both critical in intent and institutionally guaranteed', was seen to be historically confined to the period of the early development of a commercial society and 'the public' it embraced to a tiny elite — in practice, the educated, male and property-owning readers and correspondents of what is presented as an essentially discursive, learned, practical and open-minded press. Indeed, the expansion of the public realm, through the emergence of forms of working-class organization and the contemporaneous rise of commercial journalism, heralded the beginning of the end of the ascendancy of this classical model of the public sphere. Increasingly, through the nineteenth century, Habermas insists, politics can be seen to be based less upon this discursively-formed, educated and rational public opinion than upon 'the compromise of conflicting private interests' or the 'pressure of the street'.

Under contemporary 'social welfare state mass democracy', these tendencies become acute. With the growth of large-scale public and private bureaucracies, and the development of mass parties, the distinction between the public and the private becomes increasingly unclear. Under this 'interweaving of the public and private realm, not only do the political authorities assume certain functions in the sphere of commodity exchange and social labour, but conversely social powers now assume political functions'. Anticipating certain later analyses of corporatism, Habermas argues that this leads to 'a kind of "refeudalization" of the public sphere' in which 'large organizations strive for compromises with the state and with each other, excluding the public sphere wherever possible.' Increasingly, the genuinely discursive will-formation of an authentic and critical public opinion is abandoned in favour of the manipulative strategies of 'publicity' and 'public relations'.[10]

There are, Habermas insists, countervailing tendencies within the social welfare state, principally mobilized through 'the extension of fundamental rights', which affords the possibility that 'a public body of organized private individuals' could displace 'the now-defunct body of private individuals who relate individually to each other'. However, it remains the case, so Habermas argues in *Towards a Rational Society* (1971) that,

> the depoliticization of the mass of the population and the decline of the public realm as a political institution are components of a system of domination that tends to exclude practical questions from public discussion. The bureaucratized exercise of power has its counterpart in *a public realm confined to spectacles and acclamation*.[11]

Accordingly, he insists that the public sphere

> could only be realized today on an altered basis, as a rational reorganization of social and political power under the mutual control of rival organizations committed to the public sphere in their internal structure as well as in their relations with the state and each other.[12]

However uncertain we may be that the political processes of early commercial societies ever aspired in practice to the rational and discursive principles that Habermas outlines, this advocacy of the public sphere does have certain advantages over the often quite unclear call for 'a restitution of civil society'. Most immediately, it can be seen to give proper prominence to the 'epoch-making' importance of the securing of the public sphere, a development which, so Giddens argues, represents 'as fundamental a disjunction in history as the commodification of labour and property to which Marx showed it to be intimately related'.[13] At the same time, it makes it possible to recognize the lasting importance of the advances secured in the classic bourgeois political revolutions of the eighteenth century, without having to endorse either the claim that such gains can only be defended through the untrammelled possession and exchange of private property or the belief that they can only be fully realized through a recoalescence of public and private life. In this way, the public sphere may be seen to provide the basis for a critique of both Hayekian liberal democracy and Schumpeterian social democracy, without endorsing the anti-modernism of Marx's 'seamless democracy'.

Again, in contrast to the more general advocacy of civil society, quite properly justified in terms of the need to counterbalance the overweaning aspiration to power of the modern state, it is a strength of Habermas's analysis that it offers a specific, if somewhat formal, *historical* account of how and why the public sphere should have become imperilled under late capitalism. As importantly, Habermas's critique of organized capitalism, and its appeal to oppositional forces, is not definitively confined to, though it is extensively reliant upon, appeals to class and (organized and disorganized) labour. Articulation of the public sphere is seen also to be dependent upon the mobilization of a plurality of citizens and of citizens' initiatives in the face of the demobilization and depoliticization of their interests and the idea of discursive political will-formation clearly precludes the identity of all oppositional interests and the assumption that there are pre-given (and majoritarian) coalitions that have only to shake off their false consciousness to disclose their 'true' unity of purpose. Indeed, the possibility of popular mobilization within the public sphere is itself to be discursively secured, raising the possibility of an indefinite number of particular 'publics' mobilizing a vast plurality of possibly quite keenly competing particular interests within the overall context of *the* public sphere. Such an account necessarily places an enormous weight upon the practices through which non-determined political strategies may be negotiated and redirects attention towards the kinds of institutional arrangements which the public sphere would prescribe, an area in which this kind of theorizing has traditionally been notoriously weak.

Yet, for all its considerable strengths, Habermas's account of the public sphere can hardly be said to have resolved the problem of an elision of 'authentic' liberal and marxist insights. His justification of the principle of the public sphere and his expansive category of public opinion, for example, are heavily reliant upon his understanding of communicative competence and the ideal speech situation as providing the framework for the necesssary background consensus upon which understanding rests, and these positions have themselves been extensively and effectively criticized.[14] Still more serious are those organizational and institutional questions which the advocacy of a socialist public sphere raises and yet which cannot be resolved in the manner ordained for the classically bourgeois public sphere. For of the essence of recent advocacy of a socialist public sphere is the insistence upon the citizen's legally guaranteed independence of the state and the call for some means of accommodating or reconciling those competing interests that are seen necessarily and legitimately to arise from within the public sphere. In classical bourgeois political theory these guarantees are afforded by the possession of private property and competing interests are mediated by the mechanisms of either the economic market-place (Adam Smith and classical political economy) or the political market-place (Schumpeter, Downs).[15] These forms of guarantee and mediation are clearly unavailable to the advocates of a socialist public sphere, even those who will allow some circumscribed space to the market. Quite clearly this must raise the question of how the desired division between state and civil society is to be guaranteed and of how this is to be reconciled with the valued 'enabling' powers of the state. It also raises the issue of the sorts of sanctions that are to support the autonomy of citizens and of how their capacity to act independently is to be secured against the intervention of the host state or indeed of other states in the context of an international order of unequal nation states.

Similar difficulties surround the question of 'the organization of enlightenment' — parties, institutions and strategies — which is bound to present recurrent difficulties for any politics built upon the advocacy of the public sphere. Open to a variety of small-scale political programmes, to a plurality of social and political aspirations, embracing a variety of large and small single issue campaigns and massive cross-cutting political interests, it is quite unclear how systemic change could be promoted. If, as is widely supposed, there exists the potential for an 'alliance for enlightenment', how might that uniformity of interest be articulated? On the strategic issue of how the social and political goods that the socialist public sphere is to secure are to be delivered, Habermas's position looks extremely uninformative.

Despite these reservations, an abiding strength of Habermas's analysis is that it focuses attention upon processes of 'depoliticization', that is upon the ways in which politics as a process of discursive will formation or, more prosaically, active decision-making is, both practically and theoretically, 'bracketed out' of contemporary political life. The most pronounced variant of this 'depoliticization', or so its opponents insist, is to be found in the characteristic practices of social democracy. Critics to both right and left tend to unite in characterizing social democracy as paternalistic and/or managerialist, reducing politics for the great mass of the population to the largely passive routine of 'spectacles and acclamation'. Yet we have seen that both traditional liberal and marxist proscriptions show a marked tendency to curtail the sphere of active decision-making and it may be that it is in 'the defence of politics' that the most pressing task upon the contemporary political agenda is to be found.

In Defence of Politics

In the course of this discussion, I have stressed four key propositions:
1. recognition of the indispensability of the state
2. recognition of the importance of independent institutions within civil society

3. emphasis upon the procedural and institutional elements of democracy
4. emphasis upon political plurality.

In some sense, these constitute not a point of arrival but a (perhaps new) point of departure. Thus, for example, recognition of the state as potentially both enabling and repressive calls for a consideration of the sorts of state institutions and practices that can facilitate effective mobilization while curtailing the abuse of power.

Again, socialist advocacy of civil society must be premised upon a radical overhaul of more traditional accounts of civil society. Traditionally, marxism and liberalism have been divided much more by their proscriptions for the future of civil society than by disagreements as to what civil society is. Yet, as Held and Keane make clear, settling accounts with the traditional understanding of civil society as 'a non-state sphere dominated by capitalist corporations and patriarchal families' — in favour of civil society as 'a non-state sphere comprising a variety of social institutions — production units, households, voluntary organizations and community-based services — which are legally guaranteed and democratically organized' — is, in large measure, just what socialist politics is.[16]

This reconsideration of state and civil society dictates, in turn, the need to reassess the procedural and institutional elements of an anticipated democratic practice and the institutional bases of plurality. Traditionally, the presumed near identity of socialism and democracy, the expectation of moving beyond 'formal' or 'procedural' models of democracy and the wish to resist 'utopian' thinking occasioned a very general neglect of detailed institutional questions of democratic organization. And nothing, of course, dates quicker than political 'tracts for our times'. Yet the reluctance to engage institutional and procedural issues must now be considered an unsustainable conceit. For given the conceptual space opened up by the division between state and civil society and the advocacy of a legally guaranteed pluralism, it is extremely uncertain that democracy, as a particular set of *procedural* arrangements, can be seen necessarily to presage *any* specific substantive content, as, for example, socialist organization of production and exchange.

This does not necessitate a purely constitutionalist view of democracy nor an exclusive concern with procedure. It may, for example, be possible to invert the claims of the proponents of an (exclusively and necessarily) capitalist democracy and to insist that those rights and freedoms which democracy is very generally said to exist to guarantee are ineffectual *without* socialist institutions. In this way, it might be quite proper to stipulate a socialist organization of production and exchange as a background condition, even as *the* background condition, for the effective enactment of democratic procedures. It is not however reasonable to argue that socialization can predetermine the outcome of these democratic procedures. Indeed, such an initiative requires that one address practical questions of what democratic practices should look like and, as importantly, how what we have now is supposed to yield to what we should have then. Here advocates of the promotion of a socialist democracy lack recourse to the brilliantly clear-cut and symmetrical lines of 'classical' marxist theory which has been able, albeit in the face of much of the historical experience of the international labour movement, to cut through the tiresome rubric and messy practices of actual democratic institutions. For once the legitimacy of the division between state and civil society is welcomed, and pluralism embraced, it becomes impossible to proceed without asking how democratic politics is to be organized. The recent work of Gorz and of Carmen Sirianni indicates some of the ways in which such a project might be addressed — and suggests just how far there is still to go.[17]

The complex of issues surrounding institutions and procedures must remain to be discussed in detail elsewhere. But, even here, it is possible for us to address at least one long-standing conundrum, that of the relation between the 'tactics' for realizing socialism and the kind of fully-formed socialism to which they are to give rise. In its 'classical' form, this question turned upon the possibility of proceeding to a democratically-expansive socialism through non-democratic methods. The sticking point was whether political dictatorship could be the means of effecting transition to an emancipatory socialism. The effect of recent theoretical reformulations has been to render this particular dilemma redundant. For it is increasingly clear that democratic socialist politics is concerned above all with 'travelling in hope' and has precious little, despite the traditional language of 'forward marches' and 'privileged roads', to do with socialism as the terminus of humanity's pre-history. This does not mean that socialization or socialism is unimportant. It does however mean that socialism cannot be considered the end point of a democratic socialist politics. For it is increasingly clear that democratic socialist theory is not primarily about finding a democratic way of arriving at socialism — as it has been so frequently understood — but rather about a democratic socialist way of doing politics.

It is possible, then, that the single most important consequence of the contemporary advocacy of a socialist and pluralist civil society will prove to be its initiative in favour of 'a defence of politics' — that is of politics both as authentically discursive will-formation and as formally established procedures and practices for the institutional reconciliation of opposing interests. At the same time, this cannot be a justification in which the defence of politics reduces itself to a vindication of contemporary liberal democratic practices ('warts and all'). For the defence of politics as an open-ended discursive process, pursued under circumstances of internal and international systemic constraint, class conflict, distorted communication and distorted pluralism, remains, of necessity, a *critical* project.

Notes

I should like to thank Anthony Giddens, David Held, members of the BSA Theory Group, of the Department of Sociology at Stirling University and delegates to the 11th World Congress of Sociology (New Delhi), for their many helpful comments on earlier drafts of this paper.

1 J. Dunn, *Western Political Theory in the Face of the Future*, Cambridge: Cambridge University Press, 1979, A. Gorz, *Farewell to the Working Class*, London: Pluto, 1982, A. Gamble, *An Introduction to Modern Social and Political Thought*, London: Macmillan, 1981.

2 On the expectations and disappointments of recent marxian political thought see, among others, R. Blackburn (ed), *Revolution and Class Struggle*, London: Fontana, 1977, P. Anderson, *Considerations on Western Marxism*, London: New Left Books, 1976, A. Gouldner, *The Two Marxisms*, London: Macmillan, 1980, F. Parkin, *Marxism and Class Theory*, London: Tavistock, 1979, J. Dunn, *An Essay on Socialism*, Cambridge: Cambridge University Press, 1984.

3 H.B. Mayo, *An Introduction to Marxist Theory*, Oxford: Oxford University Press, 1960, p. 280; see also, J.L. Talmon, *The Origins of Totalitarian Democracy*, London: Secker & Warburg, 1952, and *Political Messianism: The Romantic Phase*, London: Secker & Warburg, 1960, and K. Popper, *The Open Society* (2 vols.), London: Routledge & Kegan Paul, 1962, and J. Plamenatz, *Democracy and Illusion*, London: Longman, 1973, *German Marxism and Russian Communism*, London: Greenwood, 1954.

4 See, for example, A. Smith, *The Wealth of Nations*, Harmondsworth: Penguin, 1966, A. Ferguson, *An Essay on Civil Society*, Edinburgh: Edinburgh University Press, 1966.

5 *ibid.*

6 See R. Dahl, *A Preface to Democratic Theory*, Chicago: University of Chicago Press, 1956, *Polyarchy*, Yale: Yale University Press, 1971, D.B. Truman, *The Governmental Process*, New York: Knopf, 1951, S. Lipset, *Political Man*, London: Heinemann, 1969, G. Almond and S. Verba, *The Civic Culture*, Princeton, N.J.: Princeton University Press, 1963, B. Barry, *Sociologists, Economists and Democracy*, New York: Collier-Macmillan, 1970, M.A. Crenson, *The Un-Politics of Air Pollution*, Baltimore: Johns Hopkins University Press, 1971, M. Mann, 'The Social Cohesion of Liberal Democracy', *The American Sociological Review*, 35, 1970; see also, C.E. Lindblom, *Politics and Markets*, New York: Basic Books, 1977.

7 See C.E. Lindblom, *Politics and Markets*, G. McLennan, 'Capitalist State or Democratic Polity?', in G. McLennan et al. (eds), *The Idea of the Modern State*, Milton Keynes: Open University, 1984.

8 G. McLennan, 'Capitalist State or Democratic Polity?'

9 J. Habermas, 'The Public Sphere', *New German Critique*, 1, 3, 1974, p. 49/50; on the public sphere, see also R. Luxemburg, *The Russian Revolution*, Ann Arbor: University of Michigan Press, 1961, H. Arendt, *The Human Condition*, Chicago: Chicago University Press, 1958, J. Habermas, *Theory and Practice*, London: Heinemann, 1974, C.W. Mills,

Power, Politics and People, Oxford: Oxford University Press, 1963, F. Tön-nies, *Community and Society*, New York: Harper & Row, 1957, *On Sociology*, Chicago: Chicago University Press 1971.
10 J. Habermas, 'The Public Sphere', p. 55.
11 J. Habermas, *Towards a Rational Society*, London: Heinemann, 1971, p. 75.
12 J. Habermas, 'The Public Sphere', p. 55.
13 A. Giddens, *A Contemporary Critique of Historical Materialism*, London: Macmillan, 1981, p. 213.
14 See J. Habermas, *Knowledge and Human Interests*, London: Heinemann, 1972, *Legitimation Crisis*, London: Heinemann, 1976, *Communication and the Evolution of Society*, London: Heinemann, 1979; of the critics, see, for example, D. Held and J. Thompson (eds), *Habermas: Critical Debates*, London: Macmillan, 1982, D. Held, *An Introduction to Critical Theory*, London: Macmillan, 1980, pp. 375/6, A. Giddens, 'Habermas's Social and Political Theory', in *Profiles and Critiques*, London: Macmillan, 1982.
15 A. Smith, *The Wealth of Nations*, Harmondsworth: Penguin, 1970, J. Schumpeter, *Capitalism, Socialism and Democracy*, Oxford: Oxford University Press, 1976, A. Downs, *An Economic Theory of Democracy*, New York: Harper & Row, 1957.
16 D. Held and J. Keane, 'The Limits of State Action', in J. Curran (ed), *The Future of the Left*, Cambridge: Polity/New Socialist, Cambridge, 1984, J. Keane, *Public Life and Late Capitalism*, Cambridge: Cambridge University Press, 1984.
17 A. Gorz, *Farewell to the Working Class*, London: Pluto, 1982, Carmen Siriani, 'Councils and Parliaments', *Politics and Society*, 12 (2), 1983, 'Production and Power in a Classless Society', *Socialist Review*, 59, 1981/2.

Chapter four

Class Analysis as Social Theory

Barry Hindess

Classes and the relations between them have been regarded as significant objects in social theory for many reasons, some of the most prominent having to do with the supposed importance of classes in political life. That importance has been conceived in a large number of different ways, but for present purposes we may distinguish two broad approaches.

The first treats classes as major social forces that are characteristic of certain types of society, and of modern capitalist societies in particular. On this view class relations are not transitory or superficial phenomena. On the contrary, they arise out of basic structural features of society and they have significant social and political consequences. Marxism provides the most obvious instances of this approach, but there are influential non-marxist versions. Giddens, for example, refers to class societies as ones 'in which class relationships are pre-eminent in the social structure as a whole' (Giddens, 1973, p. 132). Or again, discussing the prospects for egalitarian social change in Britain, Goldthorpe refers to the working class as 'the social vehicle through whose action, electoral and otherwise, [it has] by far the best probability of being realised' (Goldthorpe, 1980, p. 28). I will return to these examples. It is clear that, within this broad approach, authors differ over their definitions of class and their accounts of how the relations between classes are to be understood. Nevertheless, they share a common insistence on the importance of classes and the relations between them for the analysis of capitalist societies.

At the other extreme is a usage of class which is more nearly classificatory. Class is used, along with concepts of sex, age, ethnicity, housing tenure, car ownership, union membership, and the like, for the purposes of distributional analysis — of income, health and illness, attitudes, voting behaviour, or whatever. Here class may be relevant to politics to the extent that it relates to the distributions of political attitudes and voting behaviour within the population. The importance of class may vary from one society to another, and over time. It was once regarded as the most important social characteristic influencing voting behaviour in Britain, but now, according to Rose and McAllister (1986), it has been replaced by housing tenure.

Of course, the distinction between these broad approaches is not always as clear-cut as I have presented it here. If classes are competing social forces, then class differences may well have distributional implications. Nevertheless, classes may be regarded as social forces even if class differences do not show up in voting behaviour. In marxist class analysis and in the work of the non-marxist authors noted above, class position may be closely related to voting behaviour or it may not — but in either case class struggle is an important part of politics in capitalist society. In his commentaries on Labour's 1983 electoral defeat Hobsbawm (1983, 1984, 1985) can refer to 'the working class' as a social force while recognizing that there is no longer any clear correlation between class and voting behaviour in Britain.

On the other hand, the fact that class differences do have significant distributional implications in Britain and other capitalist societies does not establish that classes are themselves social forces. Regional differences also have significant distributional implications but it hardly follows that we should therefore regard, say, the south or the north-west as social forces. To argue as I do that classes are not social forces is not to deny the distributional significance of class divisions.

This paper is mainly concerned with those forms of social thought in which classes are regarded as social forces. Much of the appeal of class analysis rests on its promise that crucial features of political life in the modern world are to be understood in terms of relations between conflicting class forces. I argue in the first part of this paper that that promise cannot be fulfilled. Class analysis is notoriously unsatisfactory, and yet it remains significant both in the academic social sciences and in the political discourses of sections of the labour movement and of left politics generally. The rest of the paper consists of reflections on this state of affairs. It raises questions first about the place of concepts and forms of argument as components of political life, and secondly about the features of advanced capitalist societies which allow class analysis, in spite of its failures, to survive as a mode of political analysis.

However, before proceeding to my main arguments, it is worth making two general observations. The first is that class is by no means the only concept that is both theoretically problematic and politically significant. Serious problems can be, and have been, raised about many of the concepts that play an important part in social and political life (and in academic discussion of it): power, interests, rights, rationality, democracy . . . I have discussed some of these problems in other publications (Hindess, 1982, 1983, 1986a, 1986b, 1987). Forms of social analysis that are politically consequential, because they are employed by important political actors or movements, are all too easily undermined by theoretical work. In this respect discussion of class analysis inevitably raises more general issues of the relation between social theory and politics.

This brings us to my second observation. There is no uniform way in which concepts and forms of argument or political analysis operate as components of political life. Problems with analysis in terms of rights or democracy do not have the same ramifications as problems with class analysis. But the more serious point to notice here is that each of these concepts or forms of analysis will themselves be embedded in political life in a variety of different ways. We should be wary of seeing the relations between social theory and politics in terms of any simple dichotomy between theory and reality. This means, in particular, that the full extent of the political ramifications of problems with class analysis, or with notions of rights, democracy, or power, may be far from easy to establish. It would be a rationalistic illusion to imagine that the political significance of a form of social analysis is a function primarily of its validity or coherence. I will return to this point.

I

I have suggested that the appeal of class analysis rests on a promise that cannot be fulfilled. To avoid possible misunderstandings of this claim it may be necessary to insist on the following points. First, the argument here is directed against class analysis as a general project, rather than against some particular marxist or non-marxist version of it. It is directed as much against Giddens' claim that in capitalist societies 'the class system continues to constitute the fundamental axis of the social structure' (1973, p. 294) and Goldthorpe's discussion of the concomitants of social mobility in terms of the conditions of concerted class action as it is against *The Communist Manifesto*'s well known assertion that history is the history of class struggle.

Second, it is commonplace now to insist on the need to avoid reductionism. No serious exponent of class analysis, marxist or non-marxist, maintains that class analysis tells us all we want to know about the political forces at work in the modern world. Some go further to suggest that classes are becoming less relevant. Two of the classics of socialist revisionism, Bernstein's *Evolutionary Socialism* and Crosland's *The Future of Socialism*, argue that economic development was displacing a politics of class, and that socialists must therefore base their support on the appeal of socialist values. Or again, the critical theory of Habermas does not so much reject class analysis as retain it as a residual element in a more complex theoretical edifice. Finally, the 'new' social movements literature suggests that class struggle has been displaced by other forms of politics in the more advanced societies of the modern world. In one way or another, these are different versions of the claim that class analysis is incomplete — and that it has become more so as the modern world has developed.

In contrast to the many forms of that position I make the stronger claim that classes are not social forces at all, and that they never have been. Forms of political analysis depending on the notion of classes as social forces should not be supplemented by something else.They should be abandoned as an obstacle to clear political thinking. I have developed this argument elsewhere (Cutler et al., 1977, 1978; Hindess, 1983, 1987) and there is no space here for more than a brief résumé. The analysis of politics in terms of relations between competing classes usually involves one or both of two elements, both of which I dispute. One is a notion of classes as collective actors. The other is a conception of class interests as objectively given to individuals by virtue of their social location, and therefore as providing a basis for action in common. We consider these elements in turn.

The problem with the idea of classes as collective actors is that even the most limited concept of actor requires that the actor possess means of taking decisions and of acting on them. Capitalist enterprises, state agencies, political parties and trade unions are all examples of actors in at least this minimal sense — that is, they all possess means of taking decisions and of acting on at least some of them. There are other collectivities, such as classes and societies, that have no identifiable means of taking decisions, let alone of acting on them. Of course, there are those who claim to take decisions and to act on behalf of classes and other collectivities. But the very diversity of such claims should be sufficient reason to be sceptical about accepting any one of them.

The point of restricting the concept of actor to things that take decisions and act on some of them is simply that actors' decisions are an important part of the explanation of their actions. To apply the concept of actor to classes or other collectivities that have no means of taking decisions and acting on them, and then to explain some state of affairs (say, the emergence of the welfare state or its current crisis) as resulting from their actions is to indulge in a kind of fantasy. Such fantastic explanations may well be thought to serve a polemical function, but they can only obscure our understanding of the state of affairs in question, and political decisions as to what can or should be done about them.

Now consider the suggestion that the idea of classes as social forces should be understood in terms of structurally determined class interests. These interests are supposed to be given in the structure of social relations, and the parties, unions and other agencies of political life are to be seen as their more or less adequate representations. There are many well-known problems with this conception of interests, and I have discussed them at length elsewhere (Hindess, 1986b, 1987). For the moment notice that such a concept of interests may be used to peform several theoretical roles, of which two are particularly significant.

One is that it appears to provide an explanatory link between action and social structure. Interests provide us with reasons for action and they are derived from features of social structure. On this view, people have interests by virtue of the conditions in which they find themselves, as members of a class, gender or community, and different elements of those conditions may then be seen as giving rise to different, and sometimes conflicting, sets of interests. Functionalist sociology treats norms and values as if they provided an explanatory link of a similar kind.

Unfortunately for class analysis the situation is rather more complicated. The bulk of those to whom objective interests are attributed by class analysis rarely acknowledge those interests as their own. Przeworski (1986) has argued that class analysis has often been mistaken in the interests it has ascribed to the European working classes. But in general the idea that structurally determined class interests provide an explanatory link between social structure and action is a principle honoured more in the breach than in the observance. Far from providing an effective explanatory link, the idea of structurally determined class interests generates a host of explanatory problems. Why, to give just one example, do the British working class not acknowledge their objective interest in socialism? A large part of Miliband's *The State in Capitalist Society* is devoted to 'the process of legitimation' which is supposed to manufacture the 'consent' of the overwhelming majority whose real interests lie in the overthrow of capitalism. Here the idea of objective interests that are real but not recognized leads to the posing of an entirely imaginary problem: why do the working class, and others, not pursue their real interests? A non-existent state of affairs (in which real interests are pursued) is posed as a measure of the present, and the problem is to explain away its non-existence. Conceptions of objectively determined class interests may well have consequences in other ways, for example, in the actions of parties or sects who claim to represent them, but in general they do not provide the explanatory link they appear to promise.

The other significant theoretical role of the concept of structurally determined interests is that it seems to allow us to bring a variety of relationships and struggles into a larger pattern. For example, the 1984–5 miners' strike, the dispute in 1986–7 between the NGA, SOGAT and the Murdoch newspapers, and diverse other particular conflicts between groups of employees on the one hand and their employers and other agencies (for example the police) may be regarded as instances of a wider struggle between one class and another. Of course the cases I have cited here do have features in common but that does not mean that they can be subsumed into such a wider struggle. What is at stake here is the idea that a variety of different relationships can be lumped together as so many instances of the one more general relationship on the basis of characteristics ascribed to the participants — in this case, the class interests that are supposed to be represented on one side or the other.

This manoeuvre makes whatever sense it does only on the assumption that each class can be treated as a unified group because of those ascribed characteristics.

Since the classes in question do not act collectively they cannot, as *classes*, enter into relations with each other. In effect, the use of class interests as a device for bringing together a collection of distinct relationships and struggles requires that we treat the participants in each one of those relationships (for example, those miners who supported the 1984–5 strike) as surrogates, that is, as standing in for the classes as such, the true players in an entirely mythical clash of the titans. In this respect, it returns us to the fantasy of classes as collective actors.

Of course, no-one really believes in the clash of the titans, any more than they seriously maintain that politics is entirely reducible to classes and the struggles between them. Indeed, the fact that they are never required to appear in person is precisely what makes it possible for those mythical beasts to play a crucial part in the action of class analysis. Their role is to provide the hidden foundations of all those attempts to analyse some particular state of affairs in terms of classes, or their surrogates, and relations between them — rather than in terms of the actions of parties, unions, capitalist enterprises, and other identifiable agencies.

For a clear non-marxist example of what is involved here, consider the problem of class formation which plays an important organizing role in Goldthorpe's *Social Mobility and Class Structure in Modern Britain*. Part of his concern is to correct misperceptions of the character of social mobility in postwar Britain, and in particular to register the extent of its departure from his ideal of an open society. More important for present purposes, however, is the attempt to investigate the consequences of the prevailing pattern of mobility for the prospects of collective action in pursuit of egalitarian social change.

Goldthorpe argues that the limited egalitarian reforms of the postwar Labour governments seriously underestimated 'the flexibility and effectiveness with which the more powerful and advantaged groupings in society can use the resources at their disposal to preserve their privileged position' (p. 252). The only chance of real change would be through class struggle, and in particular through the collective action of the working class 'relying on their numbers and above all on solidarity and organisation' (p. 29) to overwhelm the 'class-based opposition which it would inevitably meet' (p. 256). The study of social mobility, then, is important because of its consequences for the social conditions that are conducive or otherwise to the development of the shared beliefs, attitudes and sentiments that are required for concerted class action (p. 265). Accordingly, after presenting a mass of material on patterns of relative and absolute mobility, Goldthorpe proceeds to examine the wider concomitants of such mobility, as these may be found in aspects of men's lives outside the sphere of work — for example, in the accompanying degree of discontinuity in their social relations with kin, leisure associates, etc. (p. 1430)

His concluding chapter then considers the implications of those concomitants of mobility for class formation and the prospects of collective action.

Now, one of the striking features of this study is that Goldthorpe draws his conclusions with barely a reference to the organizations involved in British politics and their practices. In spite of his declared concern for the prospects of egalitarian social change in Britain he pays little attention to political parties, unions and employers, state agencies and other bodies — that is, to the principal agencies of political struggle in British society, or to the forms of political calculation in terms of which they conduct their struggles and attempt to mobilize support. Instead, like the marxism he is so careful to reject, he proceeds as if 'classes' really were the main political actors in British society. The result is that the primary focus of political analysis in this study is on the conditions of formation and action of classes themselves — or rather of those smaller groups that stand in as their surrogates.

Goldthorpe's political argument in this study, then, effectively discounts the specific conditions of organization of parties, unions, and so on, and the forms of organization and political calculation they employ, as if they were of secondary importance. It is only from this standpoint that it makes any sense to investigate the implications of mobility for the alleged conditions of 'concerted class action' as if they occurred quite independently of the activities of parties, the media, state agencies, and so on. What is at stake here is a failure to take seriously the consequences of organizations, movements and their actions, both for political forces and the conditions in which they operate, and for the formation of the political interests and concerns around which their struggles are conducted. Political attitudes, beliefs and practices may then be regarded as reflecting other social conditions, in this case the strength and self-consciousness of the various classes — the implication here being that these other conditions are in some sense more real than the political phenomena that reflect them. Here Goldthorpe effectively reduces political life to the struggles of entirely mythical agencies. In other contexts, of course, Goldthorpe adopts a rigorously anti-reductionist position.

This brings us to my final point in this section. No serious exponent of class analysis would be so foolish as to maintain that politics is entirely reducible to classes in the literal sense and relations between them. Much of what passes as class analysis of, say, political conditions in contemporary Britain consists in fact of discussion of parties, unions, state agencies, the media — and only a tenuous connection with the class relations that are supposed to underlie at least some of those conditions. Hobsbawm's commentaries on the state of the Labour movement following the defeats of 1979 and 1983 are an excellent case in point. At one level there is a more or less realistic assessment of political conditions — for example, Hobsbawm's comments on voting patterns and the gap between the concerns and aspirations of ordinary people and what the Labour Party appears to offer. Much of what he has to say at this level is sensible, if rather limited. At the second level are the references to mythical social forces, notably, 'the working class as a whole' and its potential allies, 'the women', 'the minority nations and ethnic minorities', 'the intellectuals'.

Of course, Hobsbawm's approach is rather different from Goldthorpe's, but they both exhibit a general feature of attempts to treat classes as social forces. First, they operate at two distinct but supposedly related levels of analysis. At one level there are parties, movements, and the like and factions within them, and the doctrines and ideologies in terms of which they organize their conduct and attempt to mobilize support. Here we find more or less hard-headed accounts, of the state of Labour's electoral support in the one case and of survey material in the other. At the other level is the clash of the titans, the key to our understanding of the mundane. Secondly, there is a merely gestural connection between these two levels of analysis. Class analysis, in other words, pretends to combine an insistence on the irreducibility of politics with the explanatory promise of reductionism. How the trick is done, of course, remains obscure — and with good reason. If the mythical beasts were called upon to perform a real explanatory role, no-one would take them seriously.

II

Nevertheless, in spite of its many difficulties, class analysis remains significant both in the academic social sciences and in the political discourses of sections of the Labour movement and in Left politics generally. There are groups in mos. contemporary societies who analyse politics and act at least in part in class terms. In some cases such groups have been extremely influential. Surely, it might be argued, the persistence of movements acting at least in part in terms of class struggle, and the strength of some of them, shows that class analysis cannot be dismissed quite so easily as I have suggested.

In fact, I have already indicated one respect in which the structure of class analysis as a general project gives it a certain immunity from critical argument. The combination of elements of myth and fantasy with more or less hard-headed analysis offers several promising lines of defence. For one thing, it allows practitioners of class analysis to dismiss many others as reductionist or economistic. Non-marxist class theorists habitually criticize marxism, and marxists frequently criticize each other, on precisely those grounds. Attacks on economism are an important part of Lenin's political analyses. Hobsbawm's rejoinders (1984, 1985) to his marxist critics provide a more recent example. Those who are chastised in this way can, of course, accuse their critics of running away from class politics. (See Fine et al., 1986, and Wood, 1986, for recent examples.) Indeed, the great advantage of the merely gestural character of the connection that class analysis provides between its two levels of analysis is that it always allows the defence that any particular critical argument has misunderstood how class analysis really works — and that what might seem to be its failures are really the results of faulty application.

In view of such defences then, it would be wrong to imagine even in academic life that class analysis will give up the ghost merely on the strength of the arguments against it. It would also be a mistake to imagine that class analysis was uniquely situated in this respect. Tales of rational economic man and his (sic) more or less close relations play a far more significant role than does class analysis in the academic social sciences. Systematic evidence and rigorous argument may play their part in some of these tales — just as they do in some forms of class analysis — but so too do powerful elements of myth and fantasy. It will take more than argument and evidence to dispose of these conceptions. The elements of myth and fantasy that sustain them in academic life can also be expected to operate in other contexts.

Now, these comments relate to the character of class analysis as a mode of social thought, without reference to the ways in which it might function as a component in political life. We should be careful to distinguish questions of the political significance of class analysis (or of tales of rational economic man) from questions of its coherence or validity as a mode of analysis. In *What Is To Be Done?* Lenin insisted that '[w]ithout revolutionary theory there can be no revolutionary movement' (1961, p. 369). Now there is a sense in which the statement is correct, but it is not the sense that Lenin intended. What he had in mind was marxist theory, which he believed to be scientific. Unfortunately for Lenin's argument on this point 'revolutionary theory' does not have to be scientific, or even particularly coherent, to play a significant part in politics.

All movements, parties and other organizations involve forms of political calculation, assessment and evaluation. They provide actors with means to identify the social conditions in which they operate, to set objectives and to recognize possible friends and supporters, enemies and other obstacles, and to find ways of dealing with them. In this sense there can indeed be no revolutionary movement without revolutionary theory. But it would be a rationalist illusion to imagine that its survival, or even success, requires the coherence, 'scientific' validity or objectivity of its forms of calculation, assessment and evaluation. There are numerous examples of more or less successful political movements making use of what, to most readers of this paper, will seem bizarre and unsatisfactory modes of analysis. The very different successes of Thatcherism and German Fascism are obvious examples. Another would be Shi'ite Islam. Although class analysis does not have the overt religious connotations of Shi'ism, the two are alike in at least the following respects. They have had a number of (somewhat equivocal) successes and they have survived numerous failures. Both doctrines have means of accounting for their failures and of deriving a certain kind of comfort from them. They have also accumulated a fund of empirical examples to be invoked in support of their political generalizations. Few in the west, whatever their political persuasion, would claim that the political significance of Shi'ite Islam demonstrates its validity as a mode of political analysis. The same must be said of class analysis.

Still, if validity or coherence is not a necessary condition for the political significance of a doctrine or 'theory', it must nevertheless provide those who employ it with some purchase on the world. That is, it must provide some means of assessing situations and of deciding on objectives to pursue within them, means of identifying friends, enemies and obstacles and deciding what to do about them. Any reasonably elaborate body of contemporary social thought provides a variety of resources adequate to these purposes. What it must also do, of course, is provide means of coming to terms with conditions when things go wrong. The question of why the working class in the advanced capitalist societies have failed on the whole to recognize and act on their objective interests has generated a considerable literature of explanation within western marxism.

Two general features of class analysis are worth noting in these respects. First, the merely gestural character of its reductionism means that the two levels at which class analysis is conducted may operate with some degree of independence from each other. This, of course, provides class analysis with an invaluable device for coming to terms with its practical failures. I have already suggested, for example, that reference to classes and relations between them may, despite appearances, have little direct bearing on the practical political analyses and arguments conducted in its name. Hobsbawm's pieces on the 1983 Election are good examples. A rather different point is that the invocation of classes, their interests and the relations between them, may have a different significance in the context of attempts to mobilize or maintain support, or in the conduct of internal party disputes, than it does in the day-to-day decision-making of a party or other organization.

This last comment brings us to the second feature. The mythical protagonists invoked by class analysis are not without a certain purchase of their own. The point here is simply that, in all versions of class analysis, the specification of the classes themselves invariably identifies property and employment relations as significant features of their account of the world. Part of the conceptual purchase of class analysis is a function of its reference to important aspects of work organization and of non-work social life. By the same token, part of the continued weakness of class politics is a function of the difficulty of dealing with the growth since the late nineteenth century of impersonal forms of property and of the employment of those who do not fall readily into the categories of capitalist or exploited wage-labourer. The point is not at all that class analysis has no resources for dealing with these developments, but rather that it has far too many. Whatever else they may have achieved, the various contributions to the debates about the new middle classes have certainly undermined the clear-cut division between those who possess means of production and those who do not. This suggests an important respect in which the potential appeal of class analysis may have declined in the more advanced economies throughout this century.

There are, finally, two further complications to be introduced before I conclude this section. First, these general comments about the 'purchase' of class analysis take no account of the social situations of actors who may or may not be in a position to employ it. For one thing, class analysis would have to coexist with actors' other concerns, objectives and modes of assessing situations. A political party concerned to pursue what it believes to be the interests of the working class as a whole is also likely to have a variety of more immediate concerns. For another, actors will differ with regard to the modes of assessing and evaluating situations available to them. The cultural and educational diversity of any complex society will ensure such differential availability. For example, the use of professional discourses generally requires specialist training and often the occupation of a particular professional position. Even if discourses are available to actors it does not follow that they will be employed. For example, accountants may find it difficult to locate themselves and *their* interests in terms of a class-based socialist discourse. Or again, the modes of analysis employed by actors may well depend on the possibilities for action that seem to be available to them. While all employees in a manufacturing enterprise may be affected by its investment strategy, they are unlikely to be affected in the same way by that strategy or to be equally well-placed to act on it. For these and other reasons the kind of purchase on the world that class analysis has to offer can vary considerably according to different features of the conditions in which actors find themselves.

Secondly, the degree of purchase on the world that class analysis offers at each of its levels of analysis provides no guarantee of mass support. Class analysis is very far from being the only mode of political assessment available to actors in the modern world. Those who do conduct their politics at least in part in terms of some form of class analysis have to work together and compete with adherents of other versions of class analysis and with agencies who have other ways of conducting their political activities — in terms of individualistic ideologies, nationalism, and religious and other sectional divisions. Political support for movements and organizations operating in terms of different ways of conducting and analysing politics is one of the outcomes of competition between them. It is never simply a reflection of social structure. In this respect, the relative strength or weakness of class-based political movements in Britain, Sweden and the different parts of North America cannot be explained without reference to the outcomes of past struggles over the policies and internal structure of particular organizations, conflicts between competing movements and organizations, and the outcomes of more widespread attempts to win support.

III

I have argued that class analysis is unsatisfactory as a mode of political analysis, and I have indicated some of the general features of class analysis that help it to continue as a significant element in the academic social sciences and in other political discourses. Let me conclude by returning to my comment on socialist revisionism. Class analysis operates in terms of some combination of two interrelated elements, a notion of classes as social forces and a conception of class interests as structurally determined. I have disputed both of them. Socialists who regard those elements as providing an insufficient foundation for socialist politics have traditionally stressed values in their place. Bernstein and Crosland, in rather different ways, both respond to what they perceive as the inadequacy of a politics organized around the pursuit of class interests by proposing that socialist politics be organized primarily around socialist values instead.

Now, there is no denying that appeals to values can be effective in some conditions, just as appeals to interests can be in others. But attempts to provide accounts of movements and the conditions of their support in terms of values are no more satisfactory than those conducted in terms of interests. If the revisionist analysis of the decline of interest-based politics as a function of capitalist economic development involves an altogether too simple a view of the conditions in which interests are politically significant, then the value-based politics which it presents as the alternative is equally simplistic. In fact there is an important sense in which the two belong together, with interests and values being seen as the two primary sources of motivation for rational action. If the appeal to one is unsatisfactory then the other must be brought in to take its place. In this respect marxism's materialist account of action in terms of interests, Bernstein's and Crosland's ethical idealisms, and Weber's combination of interests and values (ideal interests) are all variations on a common theme. Stories of rational economic man are constructed around a closely related theme. In this case the perceived inadequacy of analyses conducted in terms of preference rankings provokes the remedy of introducing altruism as an alternative to self-interest as another source of motivation.

It would take too long to pursue the ramifications of this theme in any detail here. For present purposes what is so problematic about the theme, apart from all the difficulties associated with the notion of rationality, is the way it takes the motivation of action as the starting point for its account of political life. Of course motivations play a part in the actions of individuals, but it does not follow that a simple model of motivation (people pursue their interests, preferences, values, or whatever) is a suitable starting point for social analysis. I have argued elsewhere (Hindess, 1986b) that interests, values, or whatever, are effective, in the sense of having social consequences, only in so far as they relate to the decisions and actions of some actor or actors. They depend on the possibility of their being formulated by the relevant actors, and therefore on the modes of analysing and evaluating situations available to them. The interests, preferences, values or whatever pursued by actors are always dependent on the discursive and other conditions which allow them to be formulated.

The trouble with general accounts of socialist (or any other) politics in terms of the pursuit of interests or the pursuit of values is that they bear little relation to the range of modes of social analysis available to actors in complex societies and the complexity of the social conditions in which they may be employed. Movements, parties and other organizations obtain their support in different ways from a variety of differently situated groups and individuals. Rather than attempt the construction of such general accounts we need to raise questions concerning modes of social analysis and the social conditions in which they may be employed and therefore have consequences for the decisions and actions of some actor or actors. Considerations of the validity and coherence of class analysis and other modes of social analysis may be important, but they cannot provide the answers to those questions.

References

Bernstein, E. (1961), *Evolutionary Socialism*, New York: Schocken.

Crosland, C.A.R. (1956), *The Future of Socialism*, London: Cape.

Cutler, A.J., Hindess, B., Hirst, P.Q. and Hussain, A. (1977, 1978), *Marx's Capital and Capitalism Today* (2 vols.), London: Routledge & Kegan Paul.

Fine, B., et al. (1986), *Class Politics*, London: Pluto Press.

Giddens, A. (1973), *The Class Structure of the Advanced Societies*, London: Hutchinson.

Goldthorpe, J.H. (1980), *Social Mobility and Class Structure in Modern*

Britain, Oxford: Clarendon Press.

Hindess, B. (1982), 'Power, Interests, and the Outcomes of Struggles', *Sociology*, 16, 4.

Hindess, B. (1983), *Parliamentary Democracy & Socialist Politics*, London: Routledge & Kegan Paul.

Hindess, B. (1986a), 'Actors and Social Relations', in M. Wardell and S.Turner (eds.), *Sociological Theory in Transition*, London: Allen & Unwin.

Hindess, B. (1986b), 'Interests in Political Analysis', in J. Law (ed.), *Power, Action and Belief, Sociological Review Monograph 32*, London: Routledge & Kegan Paul.

Hindess, B. (1987), *Politics and Class Analysis*, Oxford: Blackwell.

Hobsbawm, E. (1983), 'Labour's Lost Millions', *Marxism Today*, Sept. 1983.

Hobsbawm, E. (1984), 'Labour: rump or rebirth', *Marxism Today*, March 1984.

Hobsbawm, E. (1985), 'The Retreat into Extremism', *Marxism Today*, April, 1985.

Lenin, V.I. (1961), *What Is To Be Done?, Collected Works, 5*, London: Lawrence & Wishart.

Marx, K. and Engels, F. (1968), 'The Communist Manifesto' in *Selected Works*, London: Lawrence & Wishart.

Miliband, R. (1973), *The State in Capitalist Society*, London: Quartet Books.

Przeworski, A. (1986), *Capitalism and Social Democracy*, Cambridge: Cambridge University Press.

Rose, R. and McAllister, I. (1986), *Voters Begin to Choose*, London: Sage.

Wood, E. (1986), *The Retreat from Class*, London: Verso.

Chapter five

States, Populations and Productivity: Towards a Political Theory of Welfare States

Göran Therborn

The Everyday State and Political Sociology

The welfare state, the social state (Sozialstaat), the providential state (Etat providentiel), social security, social services, whatever it is called, is a major aspect of politics, policy, and states of our time. Alongside liberal democracy, it may be said to be the most pervasive feature of the everyday politics and policy of western countries. Health and social care, education, and income maintenance constitute today the predominant everyday activities and pecuniary efforts of the states of advanced capitalism.

Table 1 Social Expenditure[1] and Social Services Employment[2] as Per Cent of Total Public Expenditure and Employment, circa 1980

Country	Social Expenditure	Social Employment
Canada	53	n.d.
United States	59	49
Japan	57	n.d.
Australia	61	n.d.
New Zealand	51	n.d.
Austria	58	n.d.
Belgium	74	n.d.
Denmark	53	n.d.
Finland	56	n.d.
France	61	42
Germany	66	38
Ireland	52	n.d.
Italy	64	38
Netherlands	61	60
Norway	56	n.d.
Sweden	52	54
Switzerland	48	n.d.
United Kingdom	55	45

Notes: 1. Expenditure on health care, social insurance, social assistance, and education. Basic year 1981. 2. Employees in public health, education, social security, and social work; the total of public employment includes that of public enterprises. Basic year 1980.
Sources: Expenditure: calculations from OECD (1985a); employment, Netherlands: calculations from Sociaal en Cultureel Planbureau (1980), figure includes employment in publicly financed para-statal social services; employment, other countries: Rose (1985:16).

The expenditure figures are minimum ones and exclude several social services. For instance, in the Swedish case — where these other services are more extensive than elsewhere — if we add the cost of preventive unemployment policies, housing subsidies, the running of sports and culture institutions, and public childcare, social expenditure would make up about 66 per cent of total public expenditure, instead of 52 per cent above (Therborn 1987).

In general political theory, political science, sociology, and historiography, the welfare state has so far received scant attention, if any. A prominent sociological theorist such as Anthony Giddens (1985) can write an almost 400-page-long treatise on the modern state hardly touching the welfare state at all, and implying — under Foucauldian spell — that surveillance is without comparison and discussion a more important feature of contemporary democratic capitalist states than, say, the educational qualification and the socioeconomic maintenance of the population. A distinguished French political scientist publishes a series of studies on 'The Logic of the State', in which any social service logic is completely missing (Birnbaum 1982). A major collective work on western European state formation (Tilly 1975) bypasses the welfare state problematic altogether.

German theorists are more interested, but they tend to give the subject a rather lefthanded treatment. Niklas Luhmann's (1981) little book on political theory in the welfare state is without doubt one of the most lightweight contributions by this prolific central figure of German sociological theory. Claus Offe (1984) has put the welfare state in the title of one of his English collections of essays, and deals with what he sees as problems and contradictions of the welfare state. But the treatment of the welfare state is subordinated to a particular interpretation of the post-1974 crisis and involves a confounding of economic and labour market policies and social policies, in a notion of a 'Keynesian Welfare State', which does not hold empirical water (cf. Therborn 1986a; Therborn and Roebroek 1986).

Ironically enough, mid-twentieth-century British empiricism has provided us with two of the still most stimulating theories of the welfare state, by T.H.Marshall and Richard Titmuss. Both have, however, an idealistic individualistic orientation, which has to be surpassed. Marshall (1965: Chapter IV) focuses on social citizenship rights, on their development in England in the twentieth century after that of civil and political citizenship rights. Titmuss' (1974:30–1) distinction of three welfare models, the residual, the industrial-achievement, and the institutional ones, looks at how individual needs are met. Neither has an eye for state reasons and for political power. The social citizenship reception, furthermore, not only misses the continental European social security development, which was not related to citizenship but to social status and to insurance contribution, but also the imbrication of citizenship and class in the post-Beveridge development of British social security and the latter's class-structured mix of public and private security and services (cf. Lawson 1987). Of both Marshall and Titmuss, it may be said that they sinned on the side of humanity, in a world which is far from humanitarian. The vast, and rapidly growing, specialized literature has focused on developmental explanations and on policy descriptions and explanations. Only rarely has it linked up with issues of general social and political theory, apart from an early preoccupation with the question of whether politics matters at all, a question to which many authors in the first round gave the answer, hardly. Authors such as Jackman (1975) and Wilensky (1975) emphasized instead industrialization, economic wealth and demography. That position was soon superseded by a wave of studies, intensively studying historical sequences of social insurance legislation and social expenditure, in lieu of an earlier predilection for global cross-sectional comparisons. Hereby, the significance of politicians, parties, intellectuals, state structures, and bureaucrats came to the fore.

One theoretical track has seen the rise of social insurance as a response to modernization problems of equality and security and used Stein Rokkan's models of political development and political cleavages as a guiding thread of long-term investigation (Flora and Alber 1981; Alber 1982).

Another developed a Social Democratic variant of neo-marxism, whereby, in particular, postwar welfare state growth and welfare state forms were seen as determined by the parliamentary and the trade union strength of the working class. A major protagonist is Walter Korpi, to whom the welfare state is basically defined in terms of equality (1983:185). (Overviews are given by Shalev 1983 and Therborn 1986b.) In the work of Richard Rose (1985, Rose and Shiratori 1986), there is, without being fully elaborated, a noteworthy historical and structural location of the welfare state, in state history and in the relations between state, market, and household, respectively. Theoretical underdevelopment remains, however.

As the major feature of the everyday routines of contemporary developed states, the welfare state has become important to general political theory. Vice versa a major set of state activities will have much to benefit from a political theory modern enough to take it into systematic account. This will require a political theory of the welfare state, broader and more general than the needs–rights–equality notions or than those concentrating on social integration/social discipline or on professional monopolization and dependency. It will also have to go beyond concentration on theorizing the rise and development of social insurance, and should locate modern social services in a general framework of state activities and state history.

States and Populations: Conditions and Resources

States can be viewed as organizations exercising the supreme rule-making and rule-defending powers of a delimited territory and its population. The marxist question of where the state organization comes from (cf. Therborn 1980) will for the sake of *this* argument be put into parenthesis. Hereby, states are always imbricated in three sorts of fundamental relations, to their territory, to their population, and to other states. Welfare state activities constitute one kind of relations between a state and its population. Precisely what kind of relation is a matter of much heated ideological controversy, but before going into specific empirical assessments and ideological evaluations it is possible and fruitful to distinguish the welfare state relation from some other major types of state–population relations.

The relations between states and populations may be seen in terms of either *conditions* or *resources* of action by the state (rulers) and by (various sectors of) the population. Conditions should, if possible, be favourably preselected and predetermined before a course of action and be kept from disturbing a chosen course. Resources, on the other hand, are drawn upon and utilized in action and should as far as possible be developed. Conditions should be controlled, resources should be taken care of, developed, and reproduced. In this sense, the states as well as the population can both be regarded as conditions and as resources to each other. Theories and practices of welfare states may be tabulated on this basis.

The state always provides conditions for (all classes of) the population, and the population for the state. But each may also constitute a resource to the other, a resource to be drawn upon and to develop in courses of action. Furthermore, the population is always divided into various categories and forces. The divisions used above are by no means meant to be exhaustive. Only, they will capture the ones most significant for a general theory of the welfare state. Because, whatever other social cleavages and forces have weighed upon social policy — religious ones have been crucial in Belgium and the Netherlands, for example — the rise of the welfare state is inextricable from issues of class. As empirical possibilities, the cells are not mutually exclusive.

The table on p. 66 may serve us in two ways, to locate a political theory of the welfare state to be developed, in relation to existing political theory, and to get a more comprehensive view of what contemporary welfare state policy entails than current conceptions of the latter assert or imply.

Mainstream Liberal political theory is primarily preoccupied with states and populations as conditions to each other. That is, with state conditions for individual and group action, with constitutional rules, citizenship rights, assuming the population of individuals and groups as a given condition to the state. The task of the state, according to this

Table 2 Conceptions of State–Population Relations in Theories and Forms of Social Policy

The Population	The State as	
As a whole as	Condition	Resource
Condition	1.a. Provision for the poor b. State-financed confessional education and social care c. The Beveridge plan Marshall's 'social citizenship rights'	2.a. Social security as effect of electoral redistribution and/or electoral cycles
Resource	3.a. Public mass education policies b. Natalist policies	4 The Myrdal/Möller view of social policy as population policy
Working Class as Condition	5.a. Bismarck system b. Corporatist social insurance	6 Post-classical Social Democracy 'Social Democratic model' in current social science
Resource	7 Factory legislation Conception of social policy as labour power reproduction	8 Dialectic of class power and labour power reproduction (theory to be developed)
Middle Classes as Condition	9 Tax exemptions	10 Status-specific social entitlements
Resource	11 Property and status protection	12 Dialectic of entitlements and protection (theory to be developed)
State Personnel as Condition	13 Compulsory retirement of officials	14.a. Public Choice theory b. Social services as self-interested professionalism
Resource	15 Special protection of state personnel	16 Supply-side public social policy (Skocpol, Orloff)

view, is to provide and/or guarantee the conditions of a free and civilized life of the population. Liberal political theory may also be concerned with citizens' duties, the preservation of law and order, and with disturbing 'excessive' popular demands upon the state, in other words with the behaviour of the population as a condition of state action to be controlled.

The political theory of orthodox marxism, including the first wave of contemporary neo-marxism (Poulantzas 1968; Miliband 1969), concentrated on a class of the population, for brevity's sake left out above, not figuring very prominently as a target of social policy, the bourgeoisie. Therein it focused on the bourgeoisie as a condition to the state and the latter as a resource to the former. The Social Democratic neo-marxism of Korpi (1983), Esping-Andersen (1985) and others, with their eyes on the welfare state, have concentrated on the working class and the state, regarding the former as a given condition and the latter as a resource (cf. Therborn 1986a). The welfare state highlights deficiencies of prevailing general political theory.

The table also indicates the limitations of the predominant conceptions of the welfare state, i.e., on one hand, Beveridge's (1942) conception of freedom and Marshall's (1965) idea of social citizenship, and, on the other, the Social Democratic model, conceptualized in contemporary social science by Korpi (1983), Esping-Andersen (1985) and others. The predominant view concentrates on either cell 1 or 6 out of 16 major alternatives. Particularly lacking are dialectical class theories (cells 8 and 12), capable of taking the state as a resource to non-dominant classes as well as these classes as a resource to the ruling powers into systematic account. Sophisticated non-Social Democratic neo-marxists have sometimes pointed to such a dialectic (Gough 1979; Offe 1984: Chapter 3), but a functionalist orientation has nevertheless almost wholly overshadowed an attention to, say, the working class demand side of state social policy. (On the latter, cf. Therborn 1984b, 1986c.)

To go through all the cells above would break the framework of this article, and many of them are quite able to speak for themselves. But some points seem to require somewhat further elucidation.

Cell 1.a Poor Law provisions and social assistance to the poor is an old and common ordering of the conditions of the population in such a way, that there is a floor below which no member is expected to have to fall. The view which sees social policy development as a trajectory 'from the poorhouse to the welfare state' is moving only from cell 1.a to 1.c. The state purse as an important condition of maintaining a religious hold of major parts of the population has been especially important in the modern history of social services in Belgium and the Netherlands (cf. Veldkamp et al. 1978).

Cell 3. To view the population as a resource to the state is not very common nowadays, neither in general political theory nor in theorizations of the welfare state. It is an important tradition now largely driven into the unconscious. Already the preamble of the Elizabethan Poor Law of 1598 stated that 'a good part of the strength of this realm consisteth in the number of good and able subjects' (Bruce 1968:36). In Germany eighteenth-century political theory, the Mercantilist principle that 'the number of people makes the wealth of states' was widely expounded and embraced (Frevert 1984:24–5). From an explicitly imperialist perspective, a similar concern with the quality of the population as state resource was expressed by the 1909 British Majority Report on the Poor Law:

No country, however rich, can permanently hold its own in the face of international competition, if hampered by an increasing load of this dead weight; or can successfully perform the role of sovereignty beyond the seas, if a portion of its own folk at home are sinking below the civilization and the aspirations of the subject races abroad. (Bruce 1968:156)

3.a. State policies of mass education were developed in the course of the nineteenth century with a view to educating citizens, workers, and soldiers to the state, i.e., to developing the population resources of the state (Frijhoff 1983; Boli et al. 1985).

3.b. Natalist population and family policy developed in the interwar period, above all, in France, Belgium, Germany, and Sweden (Glass 1940). Albeit in relative decline, the size of the population and social demography have remained major concerns of postwar French social policy. The current officious treatise on French social policy and welfare institutions characteristically starts with a chapter on the population (Laroque 1980).

4. In Sweden, 'the population question' was a major lever of a very broadly conceived social policy offensive in the 1930s and 40s. It was first pushed by Alva and Gunnar Myrdal, somewhat cynically used by the Social Democratic Social Minister Gustav Möller as a vehicle for obtaining legitimacy for using the state as a resource of social reform, and in wartime and postwar planning taken further by Tage Erlander, the postwar Social Democratic Prime Minister (Therborn 1986c:26ff; Kälvemark 1980). The Myrdals were concerned not only with the quantity but also with the quality of the population, as determined by social modes of existence, which had to be ameliorated by state action. From this perspective followed primarily policies of maternity and infant care and of housing quality, but also a broad range of other social reforms, including strengthening the position of women.

5.a. The beginning of large-scale social insurance, upon the initiative of Bismarck, was oriented towards the industrial working class as a condition of state action, a condition which was getting disturbing through the rise of Marxist Social Democracy (Vogel 1951; Ritter 1986). The concern was neither with poverty among the population nor with citizenship rights, but with class control and class integration into the empire state.

5.b. In their contrast to the British and the Scandinavian systems of social security, the continental European ones are usually put under one hat, as the Bismarck or as the continental system. This is profoundly misleading and fails to take into account the very different state–population relations in continental Europe. The Catholic and Calvinist conception saw social policy as part of a corporatist ordering of society, an order conditioned or regulated by the state, but an order in which the latter should be pushed into the background. Social security should be financed and administered outside the state apparatus, i.e., precisely the opposite of Bismarck's intention of state integration. (See further Roebroek and Therborn 1988, and Berben and Janssen 1982.)

10. The most important, and to this day successful, usages of the state as a resource for securing social status by specific social entitlements are offered by the Austrian (1906) and German (1911) public pensions insurance for white collar employees, whose legal apartness in industrial relations was thereby consecrated (Otruba 1981; Kocka 1981:134ff). From this use of the state as a resource by white collar groups also followed state legislation as a status-defining condition of white collar separateness, cell 12, together with special measures, from farm acquisition rules to opening hours shop regulation, for the protection of middle class property.

State personnel, politics and employees have only recently been recognized as a significant part of the population with regard to social policy.

14.a. The state is regarded as a resource by the public choice theorists, with the difference that instead of for general or class needs, state powers are here conceived as resources for the benefits of politicians and state bureaucrats (cf. Frey 1985).

14.b. The idea of public social services as a professional usurpation is more an evaluative interpretation than an empirical explanatory theory. In its various local forms, it draws heavily upon the work of Ivan Illich (1975, 1978).

16. A dialectical view of state institutions as a resource to patronage or bureaucratic state personnel, and the latter as two kinds of resources to the state (negative and positive, respectively) is put to work by Anne Orloff and Theda Skocpol (1984) in order to explain different public social spending in the US and UK in the early twentieth century.

In order to account for the welfare state, a political theory needs to be developed, in which the varying importance of the quantity and/or quality of the population as a resource to the state and to the political projects of state leaders, as well as the state as a resource to various parts of the population, is brought into systematic consideration. Perspectives of social rights and social duties, of human needs, of integration, and discipline, namely the mutually conditioning relationships between states and populations, do not lose their relevance, but alone they are insufficient. Looking a little more closely into three important theoretical elaborations, we shall see how the insufficiency of focusing on conditions in state–population relationships comes out in internal theoretical inconsistencies.

Inconsistencies of Rights, Needs and Discipline

T.H. Marshall's (1965:Chapter IV) view of welfare state development as one of the establishment and expansion of social citizenship rights was confined to England. He did not use the latter conception in a comparative study. He even rejected the appropriateness of the welfare state as a name for the system of social policy developed in France and Germany (Marshall 1965:Chapter XIV, 323). Marshall was, of course, wise in not trying to apply the idea of social citizenship to continental European systems of social security, with their explicit class institutions, but restricting the concept of welfare state to Britain left his discussion of citizenship and class unnecessarily narrow.

Anyway, our point here is, that Marshall's social rights conception did not even fit his chosen British case and what he himself used as a major feature of the modern establishment of social citizenship rights, i.e. public education. Marshall points out, that elementary education is not just a right, it is also compulsory. And here his rights argument breaks down and is abandoned, without Marshall himself noticing it:

> is the public duty [of elementary education] imposed merely for the benefit of the individual . . ? I hardly think that this can be an adequate explanation . . . The duty to improve and civilize oneself is therefore a social duty, and not merely a personal one, because the social health of a society depends upon the civiliza-tion of its members . . . It follows that the growth of public elementary education . . . was the first decisive step on the road to the re-establishment of the social rights of citizenship [after their erosion by the rise of the market economy] . . . (Marshall 1965:90)

The latter does not follow at all. Rights do not necessarily follow from duties. What Marshall tries to put into the framework of a classical theory of rights refers logically to the 'civilization' of members as a resource to 'society'.

Another unfortunate example is town planning and housing policy, the public designing of communities, which Marshall (1965:116–17) with one qualification also tries to squeeze into his language of citizenship rights. His qualification is that planning for a class-mixed community involves citizenship rights simultaneously constructing inequality. What occurs in this case is rather, that a particular kind of socially mixed housing is regarded by town planners as a condition of sociopolitical integration and stability. In other words, a certain patterning of the population is brought about as a condition of state functioning, rather than the state bestowing the population with social rights as a condition for citizens' actions.

Richard Titmuss, to whom all serious welfare state writers remain deeply indebted, underlined in his lectures: 'When we use the term "social policy" we must not . . . automatically react by investing it with a halo of altruism, concern for others, concern about equality and so on' (Titmuss 1974:27). An important point, which Titmuss himself did not take very much note of however. As examples to the contrary, he refers only, in a very sweeping manner, to South Africa and Brazil and, above all, to the treatment of the mentally ill and retarded and of the Jews by the Nazis (Titmuss 1974:26–7). In none of Titmuss' (1974:30–1) three models of social policy is there any room allowed for non-altruistic social policies. The Residual Welfare Model takes care of individual needs temporarily when the market and the family fail. The Industrial Achievement–Performance Model 'holds that social *needs* should be met on the basis of merit, work performance and productivity' [emphasis added]. The Institutional Redistributive Model 'sees social welfare as a major integrated institution in society, providing universalist services outside the market on the principle of need'. Without this being said by its author, this trichotomy is, of course, also a very British one, distinguishing the Poor Law, private occupational welfare, and the Beveridge conception of social services, respectively. It fails to capture the continental European models at all.

In another lecture, Titmuss (1974:124–5) distinguished social services in terms of their beneficiaries: the individual alone, the individual and the community, the community but not necessarily the individual, i.e., social control, to the community but not to any one individual. This distinction does not fit into the three need-defined models above. But it does refer to the state as a resource for individuals, to the state/community and individuals being resources to each other, to conditioning relations between the state and individuals, and, obliquely, to the quality (the health) of the population as a resource for the state or the community.

Anthony Giddens (1985:205ff) has linked Marshall's citizenship rights to Foucault's one of surveillance, seeing the former as areas of contestation linked to a distinctive type of surveillance. In the perspective of this paper, there is also a connection between Marshall and Foucault. Both look at states and populations primarily in terms of one being the condition of the other's actions. Marshall regards the relationship in terms of state-provided rights of citizens in their actions. Foucault (1977), on the other hand, views populations as conditions controlled by state surveillance and state disciplines, the former as bodies made docile by the latter. And in Foucault, as in Marshall, the population as a resource crops up in the discourse only to be suppressed in the author's analytical framework. While in Marshall, the population as a resource to the state or the state as a resource to a particular part of the population are, so to speak, suffocated in the embrace of citizenship rights, in Foucault they are repressed by vigilant surveillance and punishment.

Foucault turns Bentham's vision of penal architecture, Panopticon, into a general social model:

> . . . it serves to reform prisoners, but also to treat patients, to instruct school children, to confine the insane, to supervise workers, to put beggars and idlers at work. (Foucault 1977:205). In a word, the disciplines are the ensemble of minute technical

inventions that make it possible to increase the *useful* size of
multiplicities by decreasing the inconveniences of power which,
in order to make them *useful*, must control them. A multiplicity,
whether in a workshop or a nation, an army or a school, reaches
the threshold of a discipline when the relation of the one to the
other becomes favourable. (Foucault 1977:220. Emphasis added)

Foucault (1977: 220–1) talks in this context of 'methods of administer-
ing the accumulation of men' and of the inseparability of the accumulation of capital — with the growth of the apparatus of production — and
the accumulation of men.

Here, however, the Panopticist vision of surveillance and discipline
breaks down. The accumulation of capital in production involves developing, using, and valorizing resources, not just an extension of property
holdings. Populations are seen by Foucault as useful, as a resource, to
the disciplinary powers, but only in so far as they are controlled, disciplined, docile, not as they are capacitated and motivated. The difference
between the two ways of treatment is one of the reasons why little capital
has been accumulated in prisons, which after all make up Foucault's main
empirical frame of reference in this book. While acknowledging that the
population constitutes a resource to the state, Foucault in reality treats
the former mainly as a potentially disturbing condition controlled by the
latter. The idea that the state may constitute a resource to, say, workers
demanding factory legislation education for their children, or sick people
wanting medical tretment is, of course, alien to Foucault. In all three
authors we notice important insights into the complexities of state–
population relations, but insights which are constrained and mutilated
by reductionist theoretical frameworks, whether of rights, needs or
surveillance and discipline.

Welfare States and Their Place in State History: A Third Stage of Dominant Routines

The institutions and practices usually denoted by 'welfare state' consist
of *state institutions and state arrangements for directly affecting the simple
and the expanded reproduction of a given state population*, where expanded reproduction does not refer to numbers only but also to conditions of human existence. Human reproduction has two elementary meanings, both of which may be found in welfare state arrangements, maintaining alive already living human beings and maintaining a population
over longer time by affecting the creation of new generations and migra-
tion across state boundaries. This state concern with human reproduction entails provisions for procreation, subsistence, education, housing,
sanitary and job safety regulations, health and social care, income
maintenance, public works for people otherwise unemployed. Under the

definition used here also fall state arrangements for an adequate and cheap food supply, historically and in several Third World countries today an important state policy *vis-à-vis* the urban population, and policies of emigration and immigration.

The conditions–resources dialectic of state provisions for human reproduction appears overdetermined by a long-term dynamic of state development.

Over the long pull, say over the last 800 years, the everyday activities of western states have taken three predominant orientations. First, one directed towards other states, then to its own territory, and thirdly to its own population. The typical state locale evolved from the barracks and the warship, to the post office and the railway station, to the hospital, the school, and the social insurance office.

The best indicator is the pattern of state employment, but the longest time series concern state expenditure. In a study of British state finance 1130–1815 Michael Mann (1980:196) concluded: 'For over seven centuries, somewhere between 75 per cent and 90 per cent of its financial resources were almost continuously deployed on the acquisition and use of military force.' If local government expenditure is also included, the picture is not quite so extreme, but even then military expenditure far exceeds any kind of civilian expenditure in the UK by the mid-nineteenth century (Veverka 1963). In 1851, 70 per cent of British state employment consisted of armed forces (Rose 1985:37).

In the course of the second half of the nineteenth century, the state turned mainly civilian. The main expression of this was the development of public communications and transport, i.e., of postal services, telegraph and telephone, railways, canals, and highways, but also of local public services, and of public education. A good illustration is German public employment. Even Hitler's preparations for the Second World War could not reverse the relatively declining trend of military state employment.

Table 3 The Structure of German Public Employment 1882–1950. Per cent of Total Public Employment

	1882	1907	1925	1939	1950
Armed Forces	35.7	24.2	4.1	19.1	—
Administration	16.8	14.5	18.9	23.3	31.3
Education	9.1	8.4	7.6	9.6	8.4
Transport and communications	24.1	32.1	46.6	33.2	32.5

Source: Cullity (1967:202).

Nationalization of railways and metropolitan transport in the interwar and immediate post-Second World War periods, together with postwar nationalizations of some basic industries in some countries, ensured that economic infrastructural services was the relatively largest part of public employment around 1950, with the exception of the US with her new imperial military role (Rose 1985).

In the 1960s and 70s came the third stage, in which social services — health, education, and social security — clearly became the major routine activities of the state. Belgium — disregarding the Federal Republic of Germany in its first years of war reparations — was the first country to devote more than half of its public expenditure to social services, already by 1960. The rest of the original EEC countries and Sweden followed suit in the late 1960s, and the rest in the course of the 70s (Therborn 1983; Kohl 1985:320ff; OECD 1985a). Due to a massive expansion of public education and health employment, social services had by 1980 become the dominant occupation of state employment (Rose 1985:16–19, 21). In the long history of states, the contemporary welfare state, as a predominant state routine, is a very recent phenomenon.

State Evolution and the Productive Forces I: The Road to 1945

A major factor underlying the long-term state evolution sketched above is the development of the productive forces. The marxian concept is taken in both its two basic meanings, as productivity and as the organizational form in which, and under given conditions, optimum productivity can be ensured (Therborn 1976:362ff). The relationship between the development of states and of technology and productivity needs to be singled out, not as a monocausal argument, but for emphasis. It has been grossly neglected in the major traditions of state theory, Right, Left, and Center. The classical continental European state tradition (see, for example, Dyson 1980) was steeped in concerns with constitutional and administrative law, the background also of Max Weber's theory of bureaucracy. An interest in input–output relations of state and other activities was alien to that problematic. Weber (1964:Chapter III, 85) did point to performance and also to the pertinence of the technology of transport and communications, but his whole state conception is swamped in a pan-bureaucratic theory of domination. The latter was certainly a major achievement of political sociology, but it leaves the state and its trajectory un(der)-theorized.

In the first wave of neo-marxist state theorizing, from the late 1960s to the late 1970s, focus was on the state in relation to class rule, which left little room for any attention to the productive forces (for a characteristic overview, see Jessop 1982). G.A. Cohen, whose work heralds a (variant of a) second generation of contemporary neo-marxism (cf. Therborn 1986b), did allocate to the productive forces a major role in history, but his treatment of the state centers on the connection between law and the relations of production (Cohen 1978:Chapter VIII). Recent post-marxist state theorizing, finally, has concentrated on violence and surveillance. Giddens (1985) is a major representative example.

Here three theses on state development will be submitted for collegial discussion. The long-term development of states is decisively affected by:
1. the development of technology and levels of productivity with regard to interstate relations, that is, between territorially delimited monopolies of violence, and to the use of territories and populations;
2. changes in the form of productive organization, through which the best feasible level of productivity may be ensured;
3. changes in the relative productivity among major types of social activity bearing upon the lives of states and populations.

The long-term relative de-militarization of states should not be taken as a progress of peacefulness, though it is true that the frequency of wars has tended to diminish. Rather, there seems to have been an increasing productivity of violence, more destruction and killings can be produced by less manpower.

As we saw in Table 3 above, in the relatively peaceful time of the Wilhelmine Reich in 1907, the armed forces made up 24 per cent of total public employment and 2.6 per cent of the labour force. In fully war-prepared Hitler Germany of 1939, the armed forces constituted only 19 per cent of public employment and 2.5 per cent of the labour force (Cullity 1967:202; Rose 1985:128). It was precisely at the peak of the Vietnam war military build-up in 1969, that US public education employment definitely overtook military public employment (non-uniformed as well as uniformed) — after the post-Second World War superpower militarization (US Bureau of Census 1976: 1102, 1104, 1141). And to prepare for thermonuclear war makes only modest claims on the expenditure and manpower of major states, which accounts for the ironical post-Second World War development, of further de-militarization of the everyday activities of states accompanied by the emergence of a capacity to destroy the whole world many times over.

The nineteenth-century turn of leading states from a predominant concern with boundaries of territory and trading rights *vis-à-vis* other states to one with developing one's own territory was immediately due to technological changes. Canals, railways, bridges, tunnels, roads, irrigation, ports, postal services, telegraph and telephone, fertilization, and also deliberately conceived cultivation patterns, factories, and mining, turned territories from a given condition of state rule, to a resource. Upon the development of territories depended increasingly the wealth and power of state rulers, or, alternatively, from the control of which power in the state increasingly tended to flow.

The organizational form, which one major part of this technological development required or favoured for ensuring high productivity, was also crucial to state change.

The development of the new productive forces entailed their increasingly social character. Private capitalist developers played a central part not only in building factories, but also of canals, railways, ocean liners, urban mass transport, and telecommunications systems. In the latter cases, however, the huge amounts of capital needed, problems of co-ordination, and the conflict between fluctuating profitability and permanent state and mass interest in a stable infrastructure, produced a general, long-term tendency towards public ownership or tight public regulation of these infrastructural services. The interwar and the immediate post-Second World War period in Europe saw the culmination of this tendency to public ownership, with the general nationalization of railways, energy supply, metropolitan mass transport, for example in Paris and London, and the set-up of public broadcasting and public airlines (cf. Bloch 1964). The US equivalent was the regulatory agencies of the Progressive and the New Deal eras. Furthermore, the development of industrial and agrarian productivity in markets of still limited demand had been conducive to the rise of cartels and state protectionism. Where the societal power relations allowed, such as in Britain, France, and Italy, that tendency was right after the Second World War translated into industrial nationalizations.

State Evolution and the Productive Forces II: The Paradox of Simultaneous Re-Privatization and Welfare State Expansion

The current thrust for privatization assumes the character of a historical trend break in the above perspective, and not just a conjunctural right-wing aberration. In fact, current privatization appears to constitute the second part of a major post-Second World War turn.

After the Second World War and its immediate aftermath there have been no new public enterprises started and no nationalizations — other than of colossal losses, for instance in steel and shipbuilding — undertaken by right wing governments in advanced capitalist countries — except for France in 1981, little by Social Democratic governments. To the late-born, this may sound trivial, but it does make a sharp contrast to the policies of right wing governments for about a century up to 1945–50. The private automobile definitely replaced the public railway as the dominant means of moving across territory and as the center of the industrial economy. The prewar tendency towards cartelization and, in the 1930s, to national autarky was also replaced by an accelerating globalization of markets and competition.

The growth of productivity was now matched by that of discretionary income of the bulk of the population, by mass demand. The maturing of a large middle-class market is also one of the forces sustaining current privatizations, providing a politically as well as economically significant demand for shares of profitable ex-public enterprises and for deregulated air transport.

But there is also a recent turn to a more private character of the productive forces, in the sense of new technologies facilitating new entrants into and a plurality of operators on previous monopoly markets. The most clear and spectacular example is telecommunications, with the development of digital switching, commercially feasible satellites, and fibre optics. Satellites and cables also make television relatively cheap to make. Electronic fund transfers facilitate banking and stock exchange deregulation, etc.

This is, of course, not the whole story. Hard pressed public finance, right wing clientele-making, and, not the least, union-busting — behind which is a weakening of labour in the 1974–85 crisis — are also important aspects of the drive for deregulation and privatization. And the new markets created are also, of course, subjected to the ever ongoing tendencies of concentration in capitalist markets. But the important interrelationship of the state and the productive forces is being underlined anew.

The rise of today's welfare states is still, in spite of all welfare state research, an intellectually undigested phenomenon. For one thing, the enormous expansion of the 1960s and 70s is strangely anonymous. Although its achievements make earlier efforts look insignificant, it has no name attached to it, like previously Bismarck and Beveridge. And even when a name may sometimes be invoked, it is in fact misleading. For example, the American war on poverty was launched by Presidents Kennedy and Johnson, but who remembers that its main increase in expenditure took place under Nixon and Ford (twice as fast a growth)? (Stockman 1986:410). Expansion was also remarkably universal. Of nineteen OECD states total social expenditure as per cent of GDP grew 1960–81 by more than 50 per cent of all development up till 1960 in all countries, and by more than 9/10 of all growth till 1960 in ten countries, from Japan and the US to the Low Countries and Scandinavia (OECD 1985a:21). In conjunction with the post-1950 turn to a more privately and competitively organized economy, this surge of the welfare state looks paradoxical.

To solve the riddle of that paradox is outside the scope of this article, but two major constellations of explanatory forces may be singled out. One refers to the special character of productivity in the social services. The other to changes in the socioeconomic relations of power. The latter I have dealt with elsewhere. The welfare state expansion in the 1960s and 70s was clearly an expression of a decline of bourgeois and traditional power and an increase of working class and other popular power, but a power always delimited by capitalist relations of production, secured in Western Europe by 1947 (Therborn 1984b; Therborn et al. 1985). The productive forces in the reproduction of populations have particular characteristics. Manpower and expenditure for social services and social security have so far been *inversely related to overall quantitative productivity developments*, and human reproduction has also in the postwar period *continued to be most productively organized in co-ordinated social forms*. With regard to quantitative productivity, five reasons for the inverse relation between social services and the economy as a whole may be distinguished.

First, increasing economic productivity requires a growing input of education, for the production of more people with formal education and longer education. Put in individual choice terms, growing technological opportunities make an increasing demand for more and longer formal educational rational. Education constituted 22.7 per cent of OECD social expenditure in 1981, 5.8 per cent of GDP, a growth of 2.2 percentage points since 1960 (OECD 1985a:21, 24).

Secondly, the development of medical technology tends to require more inputs of manpower and money. In the course of the latter half of the nineteenth century the development of bacteriology, anaesthetics, nursing, and surgery transformed hospitals from custodial asylums of the poor to sites of medical treatment of the whole population (Starr 1982:154ff; Abel-Smith 1964). Thereby a new social service was created. Further advances in medical technology, in pre-natal, infant, and gerontological care, formed a major part of the growth of health care expenditure in the OECD, from 2.5 per cent of GDP to 5.8 per cent between 1960 and 1981 (OECD 1985a: 21, 24, 42). By increasing the lifespan of humans, medical technology also contributed to increasing a demand for old age pensions and old age care.

Third, up till now at least, the character of most social services has been such, that a betterment of them has entailed a larger labour input. Contrary to the production of goods and commercial services, progress in the social services has been measured in decreased provider–customer ratios, in lower teacher–pupil and physician–hospital bed-population ratios, for instance. The quality of social services has under existing technologies been strongly correlated with the size of labour and other inputs. This is most striking in education, where higher education, which is most directly related to overall productivity developments, involves much higher expenditure per pupil than primary education, in the Netherlands 9.7 times as much for university education in the late 1970s (OECD 1984:144). (This is no claim for any optimal productivity of Dutch higher education.)

Fourth, the development of the productive forces, which has caused the drastic decline of farmers and other entrepreneurs and which has increased the demands of performance from workers, has also, together with medically prolonged longevity, increased the post-working age population. Given that sociopolitical conditions make it unavoidable to provide these people with subsistence, pensions constitute a third of total OECD social expenditure, and increased from 4.2 to 8.7 per cent of the GDP between 1960 and 1981 (OECD 1985a: 21, 24).

Finally, the post-Second World War boom has, for the first time in history, given rise to a large discretionary income for the mass of the population. This is an effect of the vastly increased productivity of the industrial and agrarian sectors of the economy. Under democratic conditions of universal suffrage and collective bargaining it has been impossible to confine the productivity gains to its direct producers. The result has been both wage increases in the social services sector and various forms of linkages between pensions and other transfer payments, on one hand, and productivity gains on the commercial sectors, on the other.

Productivity in providing social security and social services has over the postwar period as a whole tended to be increasingly social, with public provisions having lower administrative costs and being better able to cope with inflation and job mobility. All over continental Europe there has been a trend for private entrepreneurs, for instance, to abandon their early postwar resistance to inclusion into social security systems and to demand participation, which has been granted. There has also been a general tendency, though very unevenly and nowhere completely implemented, towards a unification of the systems of social security and, more patchily, of social services (Ferrera 1984:36–7, 41, 89ff; Laroque 1980:905ff; Tálos 1981:348ff; Veldkamp et al. 1978: 27–8, 153ff, 242ff; Zöllner 1981:148ff). In virtually all OECD countries, the share of public expenditure of total health care expenditure grew substantially from 1960–75, after which the share stagnated. Everywhere, except in US, is the bulk of costs publicly covered (OECD 1985b:12). In 1980, private pensions were more than marginal for the population as a whole only in the UK, 43 per cent of total pensions expenditure, Australia, 40 per cent and US, 32 per cent (OECD 1983:17). In short, one major cause of the rise of the contemporary welfare state has been, that overall, internal, and relative productivity developments have led to extensive, historically novel provisions: prolonged formal education, medical care, and discretionary income for the non-propertied, non-working population. The productive forces of these services have also had a social, rather than a private tendency, that is, producing them in extensively co-ordinated and public forms has been more productive than doing it in decentralized private enterprise.

The Politics and the Future of Welfare States

The future of welfare states will depend upon the development of the productive forces with regard to social services and social security — whether in a private or in a public direction — and the politics of state–population relations.

As far as the productive forces are concerned, the current tendency is recently, albeit not very strongly and rapidly, going in a more private direction. With the rise of a fairly large up-market demand, specialized higher education and acute health care may be more effectively provided by private, profit-oriented institutions, tailor-made for solvent clienteles. The extent to which that tendency will be able to assert itself will depend largely on the division of the population and the power of the wealthier classes and segments. There is no evidence that private social services are or tend to be more effective for the population as a whole. On the contrary, the US, which is the only developed country with still predominantly private medicine, has the highest medical costs per capita in the world, while being below average on usual health indicators (OECD 1985b:12,136). There seems to be no sign of the inverse relationship between productivity in the economy as a whole and that of social services and social security to be reversed, but quantitative productivity is clearly becoming more applied to the organization of social services as well.

The politics of state–population relations will be fought out mainly in terms of one being a resource to the other. The conditioning relationships are losing importance. The social citizenship rights perspective never carried much weight outside the UK, and has even there lost importance, both in the increasingly important imbrication of public and private occupational welfare and in the important as well as controversial role of a large, particular category of citizens, namely, the welfare state workers. The social citizenship rights conception of the welfare state tacitly assumed that the provision of state entitlements was no more than applying a rule, neglecting the whole question of public workers' rights, duties and interests.

Welfare as a creator of stable population conditions for state action has in one sense been demonstrated by the acquiescence of populations in the face of mass unemployment. However, the political message most current in ruling political circles seems to be rather the opposite, that the unemployed and the poor do not create unstable political conditions and can be screwed quite a lot without political danger. The elections in Britain in 1983 and 1987, in US in 1984, in Belgium in 1985, in the Netherlands in 1986, and in West Germany in 1987 point in that direction. Declining concern with unemployment and with poverty is to be expected, but hardly an end to social vigilance. Recent history also includes riots and mass demonstrations. Public welfare as a social stability condition seems to be a falling star, but it is not likely to disappear. In the full employment countries the situation is different and better, but there the opinion may arise in conservative circles, that full employment has become an aberration.

As a resource to the state, the population as a whole is of declining significance. Atomic and electronic warfare makes large conscript armies redundant. The enormous increase in industrial productivity diminishes demand for the semi-skilled mass production worker. Since the late 1960s the general negative reproduction rate of the European population has met little political concern, except half-heartedly in the current Conservative governments of West Germany and France. Here again, and more strongly than in the conditioning relationships, we can locate a downward pressure on the welfare state.

All the above considerations point to a weakening of the welfare state, if not to a dismantling of it. The most important maintaining factor is that the welfare state has ceased to be a state hovering above a civil society. In Western Europe and North America between 40 (US) and 60 per cent (Netherlands, own calculations) derive their primary income from the state, either through transfer payments or wages for public employment (Rose 1985:43, who inflates the figures somewhat by assuming that all unemployed get unemployment benefits, which is far from the case; cf. Therborn 1986a:67). In West Germany, old age pensioners since 1983 make up a slightly larger part of the electorate than manual workers and only 2.2 per centage points less than white collar employees and civil servants together (Alber 1986:111).The welfare state has become a major arena, in which primary incomes are decided. A radical anti-welfare state party or coalition will find it virtually impossible to succeed under democratic rules of universal suffrage and rights to industrial action.

However, with the reassertion of the private character of current general development of the productive forces, it is rather probable, that public employees will have to yield economically to private ones. Minor groups of transfer recipients, for instance the poor, dependent on public assistance, are also likely to have to pay for the slowdown of economic growth. And contrary to public choice theorems, post-1975 developments have shown that expenditure brakes and cuts as well as deregulation may be pursued by government politicians and senior staff.

By way of Summary

A neglected aspect of political theory is what states are routinely preoccupied with. Looked at historically, in the evolution of states, the welfare state emerges as a recent 1960s–70s phenomenon, predominantly occupied in its everyday practices with ensuring the reproduction of the population, in an expanded sense of reproduction.

The relations between states and populations may be analysed in terms of conditions and resources. A state and a population set conditions for each other's actions, conditions which a government or popular actor will try to control, but states and populations may also constitute resources for each other, resources to be developed and drawn upon. The neglect of one or more of these relations appears to make for serious lacunae and inconsistencies in theories about the welfare state.

The predominant preoccupation with the relationship to the population follows upon many centuries of a military state orientation to relations with other states, and one century of a state above all busy with territorial development. The evolution of states has largely been affected by developments of technology and the productive forces. The future of welfare states will largely depend on tendencies in the productive forces of social services and on the political strength and unity of that large part of the population, to whom the state is the major source of employment and/or income.

References

Abel-Smith, B. (1964) *Hospitals 1800–1948*, London: Heinemann.
Alber, J. (1982) *Vom Armenhaus zum Wohlfahrsstaat*, Frankfurt: Campus.
—— (1986) 'Germany', in P.Flora (ed.), *Growth to Limits*, vol. 2, Berlin: de Gruyter.
Berben, T. and Janssen, G. (1982) *De vakbeweging en sociale zekerheid in Nederland na 1945*, Nijmegen: Institute for Political Science.
Beveridge, W.H. (1942) *Social Insurance and Allied Services*, London: HMSO.
Birnbaum, P. (1982) *La logique de l'Etat*, Paris: Fayard.
Bloch, R. (1964) *L'entreprise remise en question*, Paris: Libr. gén. de droit.
Boli, J. et al. (1985) 'Explaining the Origins and Expansion of Mass Education', *Comp. Education Review* 29:145–70.
Briggs, A. (1961) 'The Welfare State in Historical Perspective', *Europ. J. of Sociology*, 2:221–58.
Bruce, M. (1968) *The Coming of the Welfare State*, London: Batsford, 4th edn.
Cohen, G.A.(1978) *Karl Marx's Theory of History*, Oxford: Clarendon.
Cullity, J. (1967) 'The Growth of Governmental Employment in Germany 1862–1950', *Zeitschrift f. die gesamte Staatswissenschaften* 123:201–17.
Dyson, K. (1980) *The State Tradition in Western Europe*, Oxford: Martin Robertson.
Esping-Andersen, G. (1985) *Politics Against Markets*, Princeton, N.J.: Princeton University Press.
Ferrera, M. (1984) *Il welfare state in Italia*, Bologna: Il Mulino.
Flora, P. and Alber, J. (1981) 'Modernization, Democratization, and the Development of Welfare States in Western Europe', in P.Flora and A. Heidenheimer (eds.), *The Development of Welfare States in Europe and America*, New Brunswick, N.J.: Transaction.
Foucault, M. (1977) *Discipline and Punish*, New York: Pantheon.
Frevert, U. (1984) *Krankheit als politisches Problem 1770–1880*, Göttingen: Vandenhoeck & Ruprecht.
Frey, B. (1985) 'The State and Prospect of Public Choice: A European View', *Public Choice* 46:141–61.
Frijhoff, W. (ed.) (1983) *L'offre de l'école. The supply of schooling*, Paris: Publications de la Sorbonne.
Giddens, A. (1985) *The Nation–State and Violence*, Cambridge: Polity Press.

Glass, D.V. (1940) *Population Policies and Movements in Europe*, Oxford: Oxford University Press.

Gough, I. (1979) *The Political Economy of the Welfare State*, London: Macmillan.

Illich, I. (1975) *Medical Nemesis*, London: Calder & Boyars.

— et al. (1978) *Disabling Professions*, London: Boyars.

Jackman, R. (1975) *Politics and Social Equality*, New York: Wiley.

Jessop, B. (1982) *The Capitalist State*, Oxford: Martin Robertson.

Kälvemark, A.-S. (1980) *More Children of Better Quality?*, Uppsala: Almqvist & Wiksell.

Kocka, J. (1981) *Die Angestellten in der deutschen Geschichte 1850–1980*, Göttingen: Vandenhoeck & Ruprecht.

Kohl, J. (1985) *Staatsausgaben in Westeuropa*, Frankfurt: Campus.

Korpi, W. (1983) *The Democratic Class Struggle*, London: Routledge & Kegan Paul

Laroque, P. (ed.) (1980) *Les institutions sociales de la France*, Paris: La documentation française.

Lawson, R. (1987) 'Social Security and the Division of Welfare', in G.A. Causer (ed.), *Inside British Society*, Brighton: Wheatsheaf.

Luhmann, N. (1981) *Politische Theorie im Wohlfahrstaat*, München: Olzog.

Mann, M (1980) 'State and Society. 1130–1815: An Analysis of English State Finances', *Political Power and Social Theory* 1:165–208.

Marshall, T.H. (1965) *Class, Citizenship, and Social Development*, Garden City, N.Y.: Anchor Books.

Miliband, R. (1969) *The State in Capitalist Society*, London: Weidenfeld & Nicolson.

OECD (1983) *Old Age Pensions*, Paris: mimeographed.

— (1984) *Educational Trends in the 1970s*, Paris.

— (1985a) *Social Expenditure 1960–1980*, Paris.

— (1985b) *La santé en chiffres*, Paris.

Offe, C. (1984) *Contradictions of the Welfare State*, London: Hutchinson.

Orloff, A. and Skocpol, T. (1984) 'Why Not Equal Protection? Explaining the Politics of Public Social Spending in Britain 1900–1911, and the United States, 1886–1920', *American Sociological Review* 49:726–50.

Otruba, G. (1981) 'Privatbeamten-, Handlungdsgehilfen- und Angestelltenorganisationen', in J. Kocka (ed.), *Angestellten im europäischen Vergleich*, Göttingen: Vandenhoeck & Ruprecht.

Poutlantzas, N. (1968) *Pouvoir politique et classes sociales*, Paris: Maspero.

Ritter, G. (1986) *Social Welfare in Germany*, Leamington Spa: Berg.

Roebroek, J. and Therborn, G. (1988) 'Netherlands', in P. Flora (ed.), *Growth to Limits*, vol. 3 or 4, Berlin: De Gruyter (forthcoming).

Rose, R. (1985) *Public Employment in Western Nations*, Cambridge: Cambridge University Press.

Rose, R. and Shiratori, R. (eds.) (1986) *The Welfare State East and West*, New York and Oxford: Oxford University Press.

Shalev, M. (1983) 'The Social Democratic Model and Beyond', *Comp. Social Research* 6:315–51.

Sociaal en Cultureel Planbureau (1980) *De kwartaire sector in de jaren tachtig*, Den Haag.

84   *Politics and Social Theory*

Starr, P. (1982) *The Social Transformation of American Medicine*, New York: Basic Books.
Stockman, D.(1986) *The Triumph of Politics*, New York: Harper & Row.
Tálos, E. (1981) *Staatliche Sozialpolitik in Oesterreich*, Wien: Verlag für Gesellschaftskritik.
Therborn, G. (1976) *Science, Class and Society*, London: NLB.
—— (1980) *What Does the Ruling Class Do When It Rules?* London: Verso.
—— (1983) 'When, How and Why Does A State Become A Welfare State?', paper presented at the ECPR Joint Workshops in Freiburg.
—— (1984a) 'Classes and States: Welfare State Developments 1881–1981', *Studies in Political Economy* no. 14: 7–41.
—— (1984b) 'The Prospects of Labour and the Transformation of Advanced Capitalism', in *New Left Review* 145.
—— (et al. 1985) 'Beyond Correlations and Beside Policy: The Politics of Welfare States', paper presented at the IPSA World Congress in Paris.
—— (1986a) *Why Some Peoples Are More Unemployed Than Others*, London: Verso.
—— (1986b) 'Karl Marx Returning: The Welfare State and Neo-Marxist, Corporatist, and Statist Theories', *International Political Science Review* 7:131–64
—— (1986c) 'The Working Class and the Welfare State' in P. Kettunen (ed.), *Det nordiska i den nordiska arbetarrölesen*, Helsinki: Finnish Society for Labour History and Cultural Traditions.
—— (1987) 'Den svenska välfärdsstatens särart och framtid', in *Lycksalighetens halvö* (Stockholm: Sekretariatet för framtidsstudier).
Therborn, G. and Roebroek, J. (1986) 'The Irreversible Welfare State', in W. Albeda (ed.), *The Future of the Welfare State*, Maastricht: Presses Interuniversitaires Européennes.
Tilly, Ch. (ed.) (1975) *The Formation of National States in Western Europe*, Princeton, N.J: Princeton University Press.
Titmuss, R. (1974) *Social Policy*, London: George Allen & Unwin.
US Bureau of Census (1976) *The Statistical History of the United States from Colonial Times to the Present*. New York.
Veldkamp, G.M.J. et al. (1978) *Sociale zekerheid*, vol. 1, Deventer: Kluwer.
Veverka, J. (1963) 'The Growth of Government Expenditure in the United Kingdom since 1790', *Scottish J. of Political Economy* 10:111–27.
Vogel, W. (1951) *Bismarcks Arbeiterversicherung*, Braunschweig: Westermann.
Weber, M. (1964) *Wirtschaft und Gesellschaft*, Köln and Berlin: Kiepenheuer & Witsch.
Wilensky, H. (1975) *The Welfare State and Equality*, Berkeley: University of California Press.
Zöllner, D. (1981) 'Landesbericht Deutschland', in P. Köhler and H.Zacher (eds.), *Ein Jahrhundert Sozialversicherung*, Berlin: Duncker & Humblot.

Chapter six

Foucault: Power and Politics

J.F. Bird

I have in fact been situated . . . as an anarchist, leftist,
ostentatious or disguised Marxist, nihilist, explicit or secret anti-
Marxist, technocrat in the service of Gaullism, new liberal, etc.
An American professor complained that a crypto-Marxist like me
was invited to the USA, and I was denounced by the press in
Eastern European countries as an accomplice of dissidents. None
of these descriptions is important in itself; taken together, on the
other hand, they mean something. And I must admit I rather like
what they mean . . . that is their inability to situate me has
something to do with me. (Foucault, in Rabinow, 1986: 383–4)

This quotation may be seen as an example of Foucault's trickiness, as
damnably clever French stuff, and his work has been seen, as he himself
suggests, as non-political, as too political, and/or as of the wrong political
persuasion. However, many of his works *are* about power, surely the
stuff of politics. But still Foucault's 'position' remains elusive. He does
not seem to have a total vision, a complete strategy for liberation, visions
of a better future. Instead he talks of resistances to power, of local
struggles, and denies the existence of a centre — class, economy, what
have you — from which power emanates. Perhaps as a guide I would
suggest three factors which form a background to Foucault's approach
to power and politics. Firstly, he regards being tied to any particular
identity as the basis of subjection, and something therefore to be avoided.
Secondly, his types of political action do not map on to existing forms
of politics, and deal with issues — sexuality, crime, madness — that
are often ignored, or are marginalized, by political theorists and practitioners. Finally, he has a special view of concepts and theories — that
they are to be used as toolkits and should, like molotov cocktails, self-
destruct on impact. Theories and concepts are not monuments to be
perfected and often worshipped, but are more like memories, changing
with time and losing all connections with some putative 'originals'.

The dead Foucault can now, of course, be pinned down, his works
made into a corpus which indicates authorial omnipotence, and a totality

created out of what was seen to be, hithertofore, a mélange, and a pretty strange one at that. We might indicate such a pinning down in the following terms — Foucault is concerned with truth claims, with politics, with ethics, and how these intersect in various discourses and practices. His interests are archaeology, genealogy, and self-fashioning. The total project will yield 'a historical ontology of ourselves' (Foucault, in Rabinow, 1986: 351–2) studying how we are constituted within knowledge, power and ethics. *Madness and Civilisation* (1967) treats madness in the context of knowledge and reason; *Discipline and Punish* (1977c) deals with crime in the context of power; and the *Histories of Sexuality* (1978, 1986c) are increasingly concerned with sexuality and ethics. Finally, the interviews and the paper on Kant in Rabinow (1986) make the importance of the ethical dimension very clear, and indicate Foucault's special approach to ethics. Knowledge, power and ethics are not separate domains — although each dominates a particular phase of Foucault's work; in the studies of sexuality, for example, we see the growth of bodies of knowledge which conceptualize it, systems of power which discipline and regulate it, and ethical systems in which individuals recognize themselves as subject to sexuality.

As a summary this will suffice for the moment, although it is too schematic, and appears to be too academic and bloodless. Foucault's works are rarely dry, often treating startling and special cases, as with the introduction to *Discipline and Punish* which describes the horrific execution of Damiens. In addition he was politically involved and active — for example, in struggles over the French penal system — and as a homosexual had particular views on sexual choices, and the ethical and political issues involved in these. His personal life, not surprisingly, therefore, influenced his views of politics. The slayer of the autonomous human subject may turn out to be, at the practical, political level, a humanist.

Power and Politics in Foucault's Works

The focus of this paper is Foucault's work on politics and power. However, these issues cannot, for him, be separated from issues of truth and issues of ethics. Especially the Foucauldian perspective on ethics will be outlined in the next section of the paper to exemplify the direction in which his work was moving when he died in 1986. This is a rich direction and one little explored in writing about Foucault.

(i) Foucault on Power

Foucault's is an anti-realist, anti-essentialist and basically nominalist approach to power — there are no such things as natural men/women, freedom, rights, for these are determined by forms of discourse and types of administration. Each era has its view(s) of power and our era, to put it crudely, has not disposed of the theories appropriate to a past era, in which power was seen as invested in a sovereign figure or institution which *had* power as a possession, such that others did not have it. Man was born free, but was everywhere in chains. Theories of power have not entered the modern world. For Foucault, the modern era is not like this at all, for 'we are not born free; we are always already thrown into some configuration of power' (Rajchman, 1983/84: 15). Foucault is not proposing a theory of power, if by that is meant a view of power that can be applied universally and generally to some essence of society itself. As a genealogist in the Nietzschean sense he opposes those approaches which seek origins, essences, truths, universals and suchlike; there *are* interpretations but ones not rooted in the real.

Foucault seeks to dispose of four themes which have dominated discussions of power: that power is some possession, symbolized in the sovereign's possessing the sceptre; that it is a centralized phenomenon centred, in particular, in the state or some social class; that it is reducible to some other sphere, such as the nature of the economic system; finally, that its effects are simply ideological and, as such, false, distorted, and/or dubious. This juridico-discursive view of power goes back to the issue of the monarchy, in which the sovereign's role was to prohibit through statements of the law; sovereign law and prohibition are all part and parcel of a negative, commodity view of power. As Foucault put it in a 1977 interview:

> It seems to me that all too often, and following the model which has been prescribed by the juridico-philosophical thought of the sixteenth and seventeenth centuries, the problem of power is reduced to the problem of sovereignty: what is sovereign? How can the sovereign constitute itself? What ties the individual to the sovereign? It is that problem which continues to haunt us . . . .
> (in Morris and Paton, 1979: 70)

If power had always, like Charles de Gaulle, said NO! would we, Foucault asks, have obeyed? Society may, he suggests, be disciplinary, but not necessarily, in consequence, disciplined.

This power which operates in the modern era, what is it like? It is positive and constitutive; it works through meticulous and careful rituals; it focuses especially upon the body; it is a microphysics working in the very minutiae of the social world; it is everywhere, dispersed, and tolerable because it is hidden; finally, it is inextricably tied up with claims to truth. Each of these aspects will briefly be discussed, and then I will turn to some Foucauldian insights into the relationships between bodies and power, to a discussion of the politics of resistances, and then to some critiques of Foucault's views on power.

A positive view of power goes with the rejection of the human subject as the point of origin, and the abolition of the concepts of repression and ideology. If there is no pre-given human subject upon whom society works its controls — whose desires are repressed and whose real interests are ideologized away, but potentially recoverable — then there is no need for a view of power which concentrates primarily on its negative effects, on how some have it and others not. Power is no longer a possession, but is part of the tissue of social relationships. If you like, it is a field phenomenon. The effects of power may be repressive and violent, but power is still constitutive; sexuality, for example, is not a natural thing, a real truth, that society controls, but it is a social construct; it has not been hidden, to be suddenly revealed, for example, by psychoanalysis, but has been put into discourse in a vast number of ways; it is this putting into discourse which is the operation of power, for some sexualities are normalized, whilst others are silenced and marginalized. This power operates through meticulous rituals, rather than in some global, top-downward way; it is, as such, a micro-physics, providing knowledge of the most minute and intimate aspects of the lives of individuals and social groups. Discipline, surveillance and normalizing judgments are everywhere, such that there is no longer any private — hidden — sphere; everything becomes an object of knowledge. These knowledges constitute regimes of truth, where such truth is not the result of an undiluted search for the real, but an exercise of power within knowledge, and these regimes are captured by particular groups. The confessional — putting everything into words, the rationalization of self-knowledge — which developed in a particular context, the monastery, is subsequently taken over into the whole disciplinary/regulatory system, there to be deprived of its religious elements. Sexuality especially is discoursed about — the monk avoids sexuality by reading about it in the most lurid details, details later appearing, in a scientific framework, in the works of such as Krafft-Ebing. It is the very fact that power is hidden — believed to be only in the hands of the state or the ruling class or the voter — that makes it tolerable. The power of the sovereign was visible, in a blinding light; pastoral power is hidden, such that we do not know it is everywhere; surveillance, as with the recently christened 'hoolivans' at soccer matches, is dark, secret, menacing and everywhere; Bentham's panopticon has become mobile with the use of the video camera!

(ii) Power, the Body and Women

The body became a major focus of Foucault's work. The histories of sexuality are in part histories of how the body became an object of politics, how the issues of individual bodies and bodies as making up populations became political issues, how useful bodies were produced by tying subjects to their own identities. We can sketch out a Foucauldian approach to the body with the help of studies by Stallybrass and White (1986) and Turner (1984), augmented with some of my own work on Bristol Lunatic Asylum in the nineteenth century (Bird, forthcoming). The thrust of the argument will be that bodies — their illness, sensibilities and susceptibilities — have power written into them; they are inscribed with power; discourses about women's bodies, in particular, are discourses of power.

The basis for such an approach is suggested by Stallybrass and White: '. . . what is socially peripheral is also frequently symbolically central. The other is despised and denied at the level of political organisation and social being whilst it is . . . constitutive of the shared . . . repertoires of the dominant culture' (Stallybrass and White, 1986: 5–6). Leaving aside the issue of the dominant culture, one for which Foucault had little sympathy, the implications of this are clear. Women, and to a lesser extent the young and single, are created as socially peripheral and become, in consequence, symbolically central. Hence, in the nineteenth century, in medicine and psychiatry, a very elaborate series of pictures of women's otherness is created, with specific sexualities, sensibilities and illnesses; the young and single, regardless of gender, are also pressed into service in the symbolic order. In the nineteenth century there develops a series of illnesses of marginality, and in psychiatry women's madness is obsessively discoursed upon. Some of these illnesses of marginality are discussed in Turner's work (1984, especially), and the relationships between madness and marginality are suggested in an analysis of case books for Bristol Lunatic Asylum. Turner's is a wide-ranging attempt to develop a sociological approach to the body, and in the process he develops a view of illness as expressive, very regularly, of social marginality. He asks us to consider four problems of the construction of the body within society, each with its representative illness, and each expressing the marginality of some group — women, single men, the unmarried: firstly, the reproduction of bodies through time (onanism); secondly, the regulation of bodies in social space (agoraphobia); thirdly, the restraint of desire (hysteria); and finally, the representation of bodies in social space (anorexia). The first stresses single people, especially young men, the other three women, married or single (in general, see Turner, pp. 85–114).

For Turner, onanism and hysteria are illnesses of delayed time, of delayed and underemployed sexuality. Onanism — wasted seed seen as homologous with wasted capital — is a result of delayed marriage, increasing individualism and the rise of public schooling. To put it another way, it is an illness that expresses the decline in the control of the patriarch within the family, a decline in parental authority. Maudsley sums up the mixture of individualism, waste and idleness of those given to self-abuse:

The miserable sinner whose mind suffers by reason of self-abuse becomes offensively egotistic; he gets more and more wrapped up in his own narrow morbid feelings, and less sensible towards the claims of others upon him and of his duties towards them . . . His mental energy is sapped . . . he never enters seriously into any occupation nor works systematically at the accomplishment of any object . . . and is not wearied of going on day after day in the same purposeless and idle life. (Maudsley, in Skultans, 1975: 86)

The 'he' is used advisedly; preponderantly, in the Bristol Asylum casebooks for example, the onanists are young, single men, for whom the preferred treatment is painting of the penis with iodine. Maudsley is, to say the least, pessimistic as to the outcome of such masturbation: started in adolescence, revealed to parents and employers by idleness, the 'illness' is incurable. Indeed, solutions such as marriage are decried: one onanist is cited as responsible for his wife bearing a stillborn child. For Maudsley, the illness should run its course, for 'the sooner he sinks to his degraded rest the better for himself, and the better for the world which is well rid of him' (in Skultans, 1975: 94).

As Foucault stresses, as the population becomes more urbanized, the medical profession takes over issues of sexuality, presenting non-religious forms of asceticism, an asceticism born of an era of later marriage and more individual autonomy, that is, an era in which sex could be more commonly expressed in its deviant forms, prostitution, masturbation and suchlike. This is suggested, for example, in Malthus' view that people are happier in marriage if they arrive in that state with their sexual batteries fully charged; happier, and therefore better able to reproduce the next generation.

Hysteria was consistently seen as the result of women being sexually highly charged whilst, at the same time, for middle-class women in particular, having time on their hands, being largely idle — socially and economically — in and outside marriage. The solutions were self-discipline and good works, within the perhaps dubious benefits of marriage. Once married, a woman's sexuality could be awakened by her husband, and she was placed in a protected but isolated environment, the home. This isolation, if not tied to work and discipline, leaves women prey to hysteria; hysteria is the danger within women which only marriage and work can control, and hence men can control. Materialist readings of hysteria were not absent during its heyday in the nineteenth century. Andrew Wynter, writing in 1875, argues that the railway has driven families into the countryside, where women are left by commuting husbands, victims of the demons living within them, demons that can be exorcised only with an active life (in Skultans, 1975: 236–7). We have the same redemptive power of work and fear of idleness characteristic of Maudsley's views on self-abuse.

If onanism and hysteria are related to time, then phobias and anorexia are related, according to Turner, to space; they are illnesses concerned with the placing of bodies in social space. Preponderantly, they are illnesses of women, for the public sphere is the one that women are most excluded from, and whose entry into which is most strictly controlled. Anxiety about public space is a feature of agoraphobia — literally, fear of the market place — and of the writings of many social theorists including Rousseau and Durkheim. In the home, their correct space, women reveal the extent of the social, economic and sexual power of men, and outside it they reveal anxiety about that power. Outside the home are all the dangers of the market place — uncontrolled contacts, insults, seductions, risk of disease — and signs of the weakening of patriarchal power. As Turner interestingly notes, the first medical descriptions of agoraphobia occur in the period when the streets become safer, with street lighting, the police and so on. Agoraphobia expresses women's dependency and reproduces it; self-identity as a private person and the medical label agoraphobia are part of the same process, the same exercise of power.

The other presentational illnesses, this time concerned with the body's surface in a consumer society which has become increasingly hedonistic, is anorexia. Having the right image involves having the right body, and this rationalized — perhaps androgenous — body has become the object of a great number of experts in diet, fitness and appearance. Anorexia is in part — as a largely twentieth-century illness, affecting girls[1] from close-knit, small, achievement-oriented families, where mothers are concerned with career and weight problems — a response to anxiety concerning appearance, especially acute for women, given their unfamiliarity with public space, and the overdetermination of their appearance as a decorative presentation when compared with the bodies of men. In addition, it relates to a set of family dynamics, with the rejection of food — the means of shaping the body — as a call to autonomy and individuation, where the arenas for such autonomy and individuation are more restricted for women than for men.

In summary, and to quote Turner:

Female sickness — hysteria, depression, melancholy, agoraphobia, anorexia — is ultimately a psychosomatic expression of emotional and sexual anxieties which are built into the separation of the public world of authority and the private world of feeling . . . this can be restated as the . . . relationship between men as bearers of public reason and women as embodiments of private emotions. (1984: 113–14)

As David Armstrong implies (1983), following Foucault, anatomy and embodiment are political. A brief discussion of work on the casebooks of Bristol Lunatic Asylum will indicate how conceptions of women's bodies, operative in the wider society, operate within the asylum, madness being part of the process in which genders are constructed and reproduced. The madness of women is noticeably more talked and written about, it is more of a puzzle, and it is more about women's bodies than is the madness of men; it is endlessly put into discourse. Following Said (1985) we could say that the difference between the madness of men and women points to the marginality of the latter and to the centrality, in social and public terms, of the former.

For the period between 1848 and 1914, the asylum population of women is a very distinct one. A high proportion of the women were young, single and domestic servants; they entered the asylum in worse physical condition than did men, twice as many in 'impaired health and feeble condition'; they stayed in the asylum for longer periods of time than the men patients; they generally made up between 55 and 60 per cent of the asylum population. The diagnoses of men and women are remarkably similar. Mania, melancholia and dementia were by far the most common diagnostic categories, and for most of the period involved between 6 and 7 out of 10 of all diagnoses were of mania. However, as far as the signs and symptoms of illness were concerned, there were marked gender differences. Women's illnesses are likely to be constructed with stress on their emotionality. Whether victims of mania, melancholia or dementia, the signs were consistent — lachrymose, desponding, childish, excitable, depressed, hysterical. The signs of illness might therefore be said to be gendered. Mania is an illness of both men and women, but what a person with mania does is distinctly different for men and women.

When we turn to the causes assigned to the various types of madness the issue of gender is most clearly shown. If we take the casebooks for 1886 to 1889 as representative, then the causes of women's madness fall into three categories: those related to bodies and to sexuality; those to do with sensibilities seen as specific to women; and those related to heredity. This latter category increases over time — more and more madness is seen as hereditary — but as a cause it is assigned to men and women with nearly equal frequency. The other two categories — bodies and sensibilities — are almost exclusively the province of women patients. Men's biologies and emotions are absent; it is almost as if, as occupants of the public sphere, they lack biologies and emotions. It is noticeable that the few men whose biologies are adduced as causal are young, single and practitioners of self-abuse; as young and single they are still socially marginal, hardly members of the social and political body.

We may note, therefore, a number of features of the madness of the women patients during this period. First, around 40 per cent had illnesses which are seen to be the result of their bodies: pregnancy, lactation, childbirth, menopause, menstruation.[2] These factors are identified as causes. The daily case records describe and comment on such factors much more frequently; the state of menstruation being described more or less without exception. Second, about 35 per cent of women admitted had illnesses which were seen to relate to female sensibilities, being weak, lachrymose, anxious, emotional.[3] Third, of the second group, the greatest number is single and younger women. Finally, a large number of women are admitted as a result of some outburst of odd or troublesome behaviour. How, then, are these factors linked? How is women's madness being constructed and to what end?

What seems to be being identified — in an increasingly medicalized language — is that there are problems specific to women, their bodies and susceptibilities, which precipitate them into madness. Women are always, therefore, likely to succumb to madness.[4] How is this problem of women to be dealt with? Domesticity is a prescription for at least partial health: married women have their emotional susceptibilities catered for in the stability and order of family life, but marriage exacerbates the biological and sexual predispositions. Single women, and those who reject the female role, such as, teachers, writers, single women, prostitutes, are both biologically and emotionally predisposed to madness. In a sense, the sensitivity of women has two sides, a positive one of responding to husbands and children within marriage, and a negative one of illness, hysteria, madness. Marriage makes women as potentially well as they can be, a view which contrasts, for example, with that of Durkheim in whose study of suicide it is noted that married women have higher rates of suicide than those who are single (1966, pp. 188–9). Women are, therefore, more or less marginal; the discourses of marginality for single women are sexual and emotional, and those for married women are only sexual.

The length of time women spent in the asylum — longer than for men — may also relate to assumptions about their emotional predispositions and hence their need for dependency. With such assumptions, medical superintendents may well keep women in the asylum rather than release them, in the belief that they will relapse more often than men. There may be a material side to this fear, in that women were noted to be in generally poor physical condition on entry to the asylum, a physical condition sometimes overtly related to home circumstances. Finally, the issue of odd and violent behaviour has a number of interesting features. As women, they are expected to be odder, for they are assumed to be more emotional than men; however, they are expected to be quiet and content 'little women'. Men, on the other hand, are expected to be more aggressive and forthright, leaving women who exhibit aggressive, manlike, behaviour easily definable as mad. Without attempting an outline of the madness of men, the Bristol casebooks suggest that biological factors are nearly totally absent in discussions of men patients, and that work-related issues have a central role to play. To reiterate the argument, women are socially marginal, fixed into a preferred institutional setting, the family. They take a central place in the symbolic order, evidenced in the discourses of madness in asylum casebooks, where there is a continuous writing about their bodies, sexualities and sensibilities. The central symbolic place, as bodies close to nature, emphasizes women's socially marginal position.

There is much more to the nature of madness, in men and women, than this, but this brief sketch does suggest the nature of the tie between women and their bodies, and how there exists a power effect upon women. The bio-power that is in operation here is not some total, global or conspiratorial thing, for there is a variety of discourses on madness available, by doctors, committees of asylum visitors, Parliamentary Commissions, newspapers, which do not intersect in any simple fashion. Equally, there is no medical hegemony — at least in the nineteenth century — designed to terrorize and oppress women patients. Doctors disagree(d) profoundly about the nature of madness, some even denying that mad doctors were doctors at all (see Scull, 1979). What is clear is that women are being subjected in specific ways by being tied to their sexuality and their predispositions. Women's madnesses are expressions of their institutional positions; their bodies are arenas of power. Networks of power penetrate and construct bodies.

(iii) Foucault, Politics and Resistances

Foucault is concerned with societies in which the domain of power has been enlarged, enlarged to include individuals, sexualities, discourses, knowledge of self and others. This he sees as involving a governmentalization of the state, the emergence of a disciplinary, administered society, a society of excessive political rationality (Foucault, 1979, 1982a). Networks of power, which form individuals, classes, states, precipitate resistances. Foucault postulates three types of struggle, and in identifying the nature of resistance, specifies a particular role for intellectuals. If what is required is a view of power which provides a master-key for social scientific understanding, and a prediction of 'correct' politics, you will not find it in Foucault. Just as repression is not the master-key for an understanding of sexuality, so classes and states are not master-keys with which to understand politics.

In identifying three types of struggle, Foucault is identifying three manifestations of power. There are struggles against domination (ethnic, religious and suchlike), against exploitation, as present in the relationships between social classes, and against subjection, where the individual is tied to a self-identity. Whilst these may exist in all societies, one is likely to be dominant, suggesting a crude historical succession in which, during feudalism, domination was the major basis of struggle, during the rise of capitalism, exploitation was in the ascendancy, and in the present the most noticeable political issue is the problem of subjection. None of these types of struggle is reducible to another, such that struggles over gender identity are not reducible to those over exploitation.

Struggles against subjection, against being subjectified — clear echoes here of the Frankfurt school — are characteristic of power in its modern form. This form of power is characteristic of many societies, defined at the economic level as capitalist and socialist, and is part of a state system which has come to know at all levels, at the level of the population as a whole, and that of every individual in his or her most secret thoughts and activities. This power is termed pastoral power, a form of power which looks after the community and every individual within it, knowing those individuals and their needs, indeed constructing them, through systems of speaking and writing, through confessionals and examinations. This pastoral power, developed within the church, gives especial attention to the individual, to the state of his or her soul and mind.

Divested of its religious language, functioning outside and without churchly institutions, this power is concerned with worldly salvation, with health and well-being, and focuses upon knowledge of populations and individuals through a mass of agencies and agents — doctors, police, teachers, families. This rationalized pastoral power yields a rationalized theodicy. Disciplinary apparatuses, developed in prisons and barracks, arise everywhere; confessionals originating in the church as mechanisms for knowledge of the soul and of grace, emerge in psychiatry and elsewhere.

This total penetrativeness of power suggests special types of resistance to the process of subjection, resistances distinct from the total struggles of classes against each other. Resistances are against power as such, so that Foucault sees the opposition to the medical profession not in terms of opposition to its undoubted earning power, but to its power over bodies, over life and death, its ability to mechanize bodies and their deaths. Resistances are immediate, if you like, anarchistic, for they seek immediate enemies and immediate solutions, rather than hidden, global enemies and total, future salvations. They oppose the way that knowledge operates as truth, that is, they involve opposition to political economies of knowledge. Resistances are struggles against the 'governmentalization of the individual' (Foucault, 1982b), asserting the right to be individual, to have links with others, and to be not tied to identity in a constraining fashion. Resistances are to be local struggles, giving a new role to a new type of intellectual; no longer the universal and exemplary intellectual, but the specific intellectual, whose specificity is set by conditions of work and life — in factory, laboratory, university — and who often faces the same enemies as other groups, including the proletariat: judiciary, police, government officials, multinational corporations (Foucault, 1977a, 1977b).

The model for this new intellectual is in the Groupe d'Information sur les Prisons (GIP) set up by Foucault and others in 1971. In organizing demonstrations in support of prisoners' struggles and in publishing surveys of conditions in prisons the aim was to create conditions that would allow prisoners to speak for themselves; thus, not to speak for prisoners, not to denounce the prison system in the light of some global idea of freedom or decency. The success of GIP was that there was support and publicity for revolts that were occurring in prisons, and that GIP was able, in 1972, to pass on its role to an organization of ex-prisoners, the Comité d'Action des Prisonniers. GIP and the Comité were able to break down the secrecy surrounding prisons, to disrupt their normal workings and to give prisoners a voice.[5]

Although Foucault gives the intellectual a threefold specificity — that of class position, that of conditions of life and work, and the position within the politics of truth — it is the last of these that is crucial for him. The battle for the intellectual is not around issues of science and ideology — although the demand for such useful science is very great — but around issues of truth and power. It is the intellectual her or himself who has been given the role, traditionally, of truth sayer, the slayer of ideologies, whereas, for Foucault, what has been going on is an exercise of power on knowledge. In a strategy which reeks of relativism, Foucault sees all claims to truth as claims to power, even though such relativism is guardedly limited in the following: '. . . it's not a question of emancipating truth from every system of power . . . but of detaching the power of truth from the forms of hegemony (social, economic and cultural) within which it operates at the present time' (1977a: 14).

In that this is not a total strategy — there is no such thing — but a series of local struggles, a series of resistances to processes of normalization, we have a number of local battles over truth, without any general claims to total knowledge or total truth. The aim? To resist, to be temporarily free from the bureaucrat and the discursive police.

(iv)　Critiques of Foucault

Before looking at some of Foucault's later work on the relationships between politics and ethics, we can outline some possible critiques of his views on power and politics. We might present such a critique through the work of two completely different critics — Walzer (1986) who sees Foucault as insufficiently essentialist — for Walzer, power is grounded and centred — and Wickham, who sees him as presenting a lingering essentialism which needs to be expunged (1986).

For Walzer, Foucault is guilty of a range of sins and omissions. His sins include relativism, for he gives us no political stance, and functionalism, in seeing local forms of discipline and regulation as functional to the larger system. His omissions include ignoring the liberal, democratic state as a guarantor of limitations on disciplinary power, and in not realizing that he is, in fact, a reconstructed pluralist. So '[Foucault] is concerned not with the dispersion of power to the extremities of the political system, but with its exercise at the extremities' (Walzer, 1986: 54). Foucault's account of things is conservative: '. . . his account does appear to have conservative implications; at least (and this is not the same thing), it has anti-Leninist implications . . . Foucault is not a good revolutionary' (p. 54).

It is difficult to deal with this as a critique, for Foucault and Walzer disagree and are different; the divide over which they might discourse is very wide indeed, and is made up of two irreconcilable politics. If we stand on the Foucault side we can rebut Walzer in the following terms: Foucault is not a pluralist for he denies a centre from which power comes; there is, as such, no identifiable political system. For similar reasons, he is not a functionalist, for there is no system which local strategies of power serve to maintain. He is not a relativist either, in that there *are* criteria which constitute some activities as 'bad'. So, talking of sexual choices, Foucault says that rape will always be unacceptable (1982b: 12); talking of his involvement with GIP he says: 'The ultimate goal of our interventions was not to extend visiting rights . . . or to procure flush toilets . . . but to question the social and moral distinction between the innocent and the guilty' (Bouchard, 1977: 277).

These might not be criteria with which Walzer would agree — perhaps they are too ethically grounded to be politically relevant — but they *are* criteria. As we shall see below, other criteria are introduced in the ethical sphere, in particular, '. . . couldn't everyone's life become a work of art . . . one should create one's life by giving style to it through long practice and daily work' (Foucault, in Rabinow, 1986: 350, 351). Walzer's claim is that, by denying the role of a directing centre, radical politics is robbed of its object. Surely, this is not correct, a *type* of radical politics may be so robbed, but why radical politics as such? Surely Foucault's point is that it is precisely the idea of a centre that has severely blinkered radical political action, especially that variety which sees the centre as an economic/class centre. In such an analysis, what is the role for women, and for gays? For local community action? For those, the majority, whose consciousness lags behind that of the vanguard party? If these groups have a role it is peripheral — as followers, or groups whose problems will be dealt with after those of other, more important, social forces. Walzer's view that we require a positive evaluation of the liberal democratic system is somewhat odd in the context of the debate about radical politics, especially in an era when many — for example E.P. Thompson (1985, for example) — are starting to chart its demise, and assert its contingent relationship to capitalism (for example, Jessop, 1978).

Wickham's view is that Foucault is guilty, as he is also for Keat (1986), of a residual essentialism. He has not given up completely —

although the logic of his position is that he should have done so — the ideal of global sites of struggle of which local struggles are effects. He has not accepted the full implications of the idea that 'the social is a dispersed plurality of practices which have no constant principle or centre' (Counihan, in Wickham, 1986: 160). If there are global sites for Wickham — he suggests the World Bank and the nuclear war machine — they are only ever conglomerations of local ones; they are 'specific intersections of practices around specific operational policies which are granted the status of "global" because of a number of other sites which they reproduce or repeat' (1986: 162). There is, of course, lurking essentialism here, which the words 'reproduce' and 'repeat' only serve to disguise.

For Wickham essentialism must be abandoned as a fight against a ghostly apparition, whilst for Walzer essentialism is the foundation for politics. Progressive politics must be founded upon the idea of better societies and better people. Foucault's positions — criteria for excluded sexualities, and for political struggles in prisons; views upon ethical self-fashioning — are essentialist. They draw the wrath of Walzer for referring to the wrong things, and of Wickham for referring to illusory things. If Foucault has shifted his position since the heady days of structuralist and post-structuralist assassinations of the human subject, then so be it. Perhaps his journey *is* from theoretical anti-humanism to political and ethical humanism. The extent of the change — if that is what it is — will become evident below.

Ethics and the Historical Ontology of Ourselves

In an interview given in 1976, Foucault identified the themes of the planned six volumes of the history of sexuality. These were to be the four strategic unities identified in the first volume (English publication, 1978) — female sexuality, centring on the family, the child and hysteria; the sexuality of children, in particular the education of sexuality; procreative behaviour, with the emphasis on fertility and birth control; and the study of the perversions. In addition, there was to be a volume treating the issues of race and population. After a long wait, two volumes were published as Foucault lay dying (1986a and 1986b), and they did not treat these issues at all, but were concerned with sexuality in ancient Greece and Rome. In part, the shift was in order to reveal the roots of our anxieties about sexuality, the basis of a science of sexuality in which all pleasure is sexually coded. However, bigger things were at stake, for Foucault had, in his later works generally, moved to a consideration of reason — in a debate about Kant's views on enlightenment — and of ethics, in particular that part which treats, not people's actual behaviour, but the self's relationship to itself, that is, 'how the individual is supposed to constitute himself as a moral subject of his own actions' (in Rabinow, 1986: 352).

Ethics is one of the three axes of an historical ontology of ourself, the others being knowledge and power. There are, therefore, three questions that Foucault is endeavouring to answer, all focused upon the subject: 'How are we constituted as subjects of our own knowledge? How are we constituted as subjects who exercise or submit to power? How are we constituted as moral subjects of our own actions?' (Rabinow, 1986: 49).

The study of ethics — and the historical shift from the seventeenth and eighteenth centuries to ancient Greece and Rome — is, in part, practical. In order to study modern sexuality, knowledge, power and self would have to be studied simultaneously, whilst the study of Greece allows an easier singling out of ethics (see Davidson, in Hoy, 1986: 230–1). In part it is a tactical shift, in order to study a period in which the self was not defined primarily by reference to sexuality. Also, the shift is political in inspiration, for techniques of the self in the ancient world were closer to those that Foucault finds appealing — although he does not suggest a return to Greece — in that self-fashioning is an ascetic, artistic and more total activity. Perhaps the key here is Foucault's views on sexuality, suggested in the following exchange:

Q: So sex was not separated from other pleasures. It was inscribed in the centre of cities. It was public; it served a purpose . . .

MF: That's right. Sexuality was obviously considered a social pleasure for the Greeks and Romans. What is interesting about male homosexuality today — this has apparently been the case of female homosexuals for some time — is that their sexual relations are immediately translated into social relations and the social relations are understood as sexual relations. For the Greeks and Romans, in a different fashion, sexual relations were located within social relations in the widest sense of the term. The baths were a place of sociality that included sexual relations. (Rabinow, 1986: 251–2)

This is reminiscent of the passage quoted in Morris and Paton (1979: 73), where Foucault discusses the way our pleasures are sexually normed and coded, and concludes: 'we should rather tend towards a desexualization, towards a general economy of pleasure which is not sexually normed.'

Again, the concern with desexualisation and with reciprocity in relationships is crucial to Foucault:

Are we able to have an ethics of acts and pleasures which would be able to take into account the pleasure of the other? Is the pleasure of the other something which can be integrated in our pleasure, without reference either to law, marriage, to I don't know what? (Rabinow, 1986: 346)

This would not be a return to Greece — Greece merely defamiliarizes the present — for love of boys and women was non-reciprocal, and only that of friends reciprocal. Now friendship may be reciprocal but it is seen, frequently, as sexual. Law, marriage, manuals of sexuality are all aspects of power to be resisted.

Forced, as gay, into a sexually normed identity — into a life that is all and only sexuality[6] — Foucault seeks a less sexualized ethic. Relate to oneself *not* as a sexual object or subject, but as a creator of one's life as a work of art in all areas:

> We have hardly any remnant of the idea in our society, that the principal work of art which one has to take care of, the main area to which one must apply aesthetic values, is oneself, one's life, one's existence.

As Foucault stresses this is not a Christian or Californian cult of the self — neither is the self to be renounced, nor is the true self to be discovered and developed by personal growth. Rather, we must aspire to, as Weber argued, 'a form of critical historicism [as] the only road to preserving reason and the obligation . . . to forge an ascetic ethic of scientific and political responsibility as the highest duty of the mature intellectual' (Introduction, in Rabinow, 1986:27). Thus, for Foucault, reason and critique are not abandoned — although the necessity and dangers of the former are recognized — so that:

> [our ethical task] requires work on our limits, that is, a patient labour giving form to our impatience of liberty, and, . . . at every moment, step by step, one must confront what one is thinking and saying with what one is doing, with what one is . . . The key to the personal poetic attitude of a philosopher is not to be sought in his ideas, as if it could be deduced from them, but rather in his philosophy-as-life, in his philosophical life, his ethos. (Foucault, in Rabinow, 1986: 50 and 374)

Conclusion

Foucault's was a developing project whose final form, if final it was to be, was beginning to be evident at the time of his death. This final form was an historical ontology of ourselves, founded upon his archaeological, genealogical and ethical studies; studies of how the self is fashioned and how selves fashion themselves. If there are problems specific to these three dimensions of his ontology, then these are relativism, power and sexuality respectively. These problems are intimately interrelated.

In the realm of power, Foucault has set out to destroy the negative, commodity view. Power may repress and control but, predominantly, it is constitutive, producing subjects, disciplines, sexualities and suchlike. Power and resistances go together, and I have argued that this does not make Foucault's views on politics conservative. There is no ultimate liberation, but local resistances and struggles. If there is no total strategy then where are we to stand? As personal life is increasingly not regulated by moral imperatives and codes of prohibition, then relativism appears to slip in, asking us to make all judgement contextual. Foucault's reaction to this is an aesthetics of existence, with the beautiful life seen as a work of art. As politics and science are vocations for Weber (Gerth and Mills, 1964, Foucault, 1978), so for Foucault life is itself a vocation. As he argues in a late interview (Rabinow, 1986:371–3) only with Descartes is the search for morality and the search for truth separated, such that an immoral person can accede to truth, even a lascivious, self-indulgent and manipulative one. For Foucault, an aesthetics of existence provides a basis for reforging links between truth and morality.

Finally sexuality, where the issues of choice, morality and truth are so often invoked. Sexuality was Foucault's special problem, for being gay he was tied to a sexualized identity in which the whole of life was seen as sexual. This was, of course, an exercise of power, constructing sexually normed identities into which the whole of a person's life is collapsed. The problem, therefore, is sexual diversity — how to avoid the self-denying of the flesh of Christianity, and the taxonomies of perversity developed by the Victorians. As Weeks puts it, in a manner close to Foucault's:

> can each desire be equally valid; should each minute subdivision of desire be the basis of a sexual and possibly social identity; is each political identity of equal weight in the corridors of sexual politics, let alone wider politics? Sex, where is your morality? the moral authoritarian can cry. Sex, where are your subtle distinctions? the weary liberal might whisper. (1985:213–14)

Weeks seeks to develop a strategics of sexual diversity not orientated to sexual acts — what you can and cannot do to self and others — but to four related issues: choices, social relationships, meaning, and context. These four form a calculus of sexual possibilities, but one that is not, as most libertarian and authoritarian systems have been, based upon taxonomies of allowed and forbidden acts. The interaction between choices and social relationships is crucial here. Foucault (1982b) emphasizes that we should have the liberty to manifest sexual choices or not to manifest them. That liberty relates to the social relationships in which choices are made. Weeks presents a strong version of this position: ' . . . we should start with an assumption of the merits of an activity unless the relationship in which it is embedded can be shown to be harmful or oppressive' (1985:218).

In the correct relationships some forbidden sexualities will be acceptable, will be moral, ethical and beautiful, but '[within] a general economy of pleasure which is not [simply] sexually normed' (Morris and Paton, 1979:73). In terms of meaning, no erotic act or choice has an intrinsic meaning, but such subjective feelings are a crucial part in deciding their merits. It is the context which provides the basis for such meanings; 'the decisive factor is an awareness of context, of the situation in which choices are made' (Weeks, 1985:219). Power operates to define sexualities as normal and abnormal; resistance to power struggles to develop new relationships and meanings, to celebrate pleasure 'in the context of new codes and of new types of relationship' (1985:245).

Notes

1 I understand that there are now increasing numbers of cases of anorexia amongst men.
2 It is worth noting that certain aspects of female sexuality — nymphomania — are entirely absent from the casebooks.
3 These susceptibilities are treated separately from the biological and sexual predispositions, and exist independently.
4 The women in Bristol Lunatic Asylum were primarily working-class, it being a pauper asylum. Whether susceptibilities were identified with greater frequency amongst middle-class women, is open to debate.
5 The Groupe Information d'Asile, to represent patients from mental hospitals, was established in 1971.
6 In this context, we can note Foucualt's comments on gay literature (1982b). Such literature focuses upon courtship, which is socially circumscribed, and underplays sex, which is socially permitted.

References

Armstrong, D. (1983) *The Political Anatomy of the Body*, London: Cambridge University Press.
Bouchard, D. (1977) *Language, Countermemory and Practice*, London: Blackwell.
Dreyfus, H.L. and Rabinow, P. (1982) *Michel Foucault: beyond structuralism and hermeneutics*, London: Harvester Press.
Durkheim, E. (1966) *Suicide*, London: Routledge & Kegan Paul.
Foucault, M. (1967) *Madness and Civilisation*, London: Tavistock.
—— (1977a) 'The Political Functions of the Intellectual', *Radical Philosophy*, 17:12–14.
—— (1977b) 'Intellectuals and Power', in Bouchard, D. *Language, Countermemory and Practice*, pp. 205–17.
—— (1977c) *Discipline and Punish*, London: Allen Lane.
—— (1978) *The History of Sexuality*, Volume 1, London: Allen Lane.
—— (1979) 'Governmentality', *Ideology and Consciousness*, 6:5–21.
—— (1982a) 'The Subject and Power', *Afterword*, in Dreyfus, H.L. and Rabinow, P. *Michel Foucault*, pp. 208–26.

—— (1982b) 'Sexual Choice, Sexual Acts: an interview with Michel Foucault', *Salmagundi*, 1982-83, 58/59:10-24.
—— (1986a) *L'Usage des Plaisirs*, Paris: Gallimard.
—— (1986b) *Le Souci de Soi*, Paris: Gallimard.
—— (1986c) *The Use of Pleasure; The History of Sexuality*, Volume 2, London: Viking.
Gane, M. (1986) *Towards a Critique of Foucault*, London: Routledge & Kegan Paul.
Gerth, H. and Mills, C.W. (1964) *From Max Weber*, London: Routledge & Kegan Paul.
Hoy, D.C. (1986) *Foucault: a critical reader*, London: Blackwell.
Jessop, B. (1978) 'Capitalism and Democracy: the best possible political shell', in Littlejohn, G. et al., 1978, *Power and the State*, pp. 10-51.
Keat, R. (1986) 'The Human Body in Social Theory: Reich, Foucault and the repressive hypothesis', *Radical Philosophy*, 42:24-32.
Littlejohn, G. (1978) et al. *Power and the State*, London: Croom Helm.
Morris, M. and Paton, P. (1979) *Power, Truth, Strategy*, Sydney: Feral Publications.
Rabinow, P. (1986) *A Foucault Reader*, London: Penguin.
Rajchman, J. (1983/84) 'The Story of Foucault's History', *Social Text*, Winter:3-24.
Runciman, W.C. (1978) *Weber: selections in translation*, London: Cambridge University Press
Said, E. (1985) *Orientalism*, London: Penguin.
Scull, A. (1979) *Museums of Madness*, London: Allen Lane.
Skultans, V. (1975) *Madness and Morals: ideas on insanity in the nineteenth century*, London: Routledge & Kegan Paul.
Stallybrass, P. and White, A. (1986) *The Politics and Poetics of Transgression*, London: Methuen.
Thompson, E.P. (1985) *Double Exposure*, London: Merlin.
Turner, B. (1984) *The Body and Society*, London: Blackwell.
Walzer, M. (1986) 'The Politics of Michel Foucault', in Hoy, D.C., 1986, *Foucault*, pp. 51-68.
Weber, M. (1964) 'Science as a Vocation', in Gerth, H. and Mills, C.W., 1964, *From Max Weber*, pp. 129-56.
Weber, M. (1978) 'Politics as a Vocation', in Runciman, W.E., 1978, *Weber: selections in translation*, pp. 209-25.
Weeks, J. (1985) *Sexuality and its Discontents*, London: Routledge & Kegan Paul.
Wickham, G. (1986) 'Power and Power Analysis: beyond Foucault?' in Gane, M., 1986, *Towards a Critique of Foucault*, pp. 149-79

Chapter seven

Women, Welfare and the Politics of Need Interpretation

Nancy Fraser

What some writers are calling 'the coming welfare wars' will be largely wars about, even against, women. Because women comprise the overwhelming majority of social welfare program recipients and employees, women and women's needs will be the principal stakes in the battles over social spending likely to dominate national politics in the coming period. Moreover, the welfare wars will not be limited to the tenure of Reagan or even of Reaganism. On the contrary, they will be protracted wars both in time and in space. What James O'Connor (1973) theorized nearly 15 years ago as 'the fiscal crisis of the state' is a long-term, structural phenomenon of international proportions. Not just the US, but every late-capitalist welfare state in Western Europe and North America is facing some version of it. And the fiscal crisis of the welfare state coincides everywhere with a second long-term, structural tendency: the feminization of poverty. This is Diana Pearce's (1979) term for the rapidly increasing proportion of women in the adult poverty population, an increase tied to, *inter alia*, the rise in 'female-headed households.' In the US, this trend is so pronounced and so steep that analysts project that, should it continue, the poverty population will consist entirely of women and their children before the year 2000 (Ehrenreich and Fox Piven 1984).

This conjunction of the fiscal crisis of the state and the feminization of poverty suggests that struggles around social welfare will and should become increasingly focal for feminists. But such struggles raise a great many problems. Some of these, like the following, can be thought of as structural. On the one hand, increasing numbers of women depend directly for their livelihoods on social-welfare programs; and many others benefit indirectly, since the existence of even a minimal and inadequate 'safety net' increases the leverage of women who are economically dependent on individual men. Thus, feminists have no choice but to oppose social-welfare cuts. On the other hand, economists like Pearce (1979), Nancy Barrett (1984) and Steven Erie, Martin Rein and Barbara Wiget (1983) have shown that programs like Aid to Families with Dependent Children actually institutionalize the feminization of poverty. The benefits they provide are system-conforming ones which reinforce rather than challenge basic structural inequalities. Thus, feminists cannot simply support existing social-welfare programs. To use the suggestive but ultimately too simple terms popularized by Carol Brown (1981): If to eliminate or to reduce welfare is to bolster 'private patriarchy,' then simply to defend it is to consolidate 'public patriarchy.'[1]

Feminists also face a second set of problems in the coming welfare wars. These problems, seemingly more ideological and less structural than the first set, arise from the typical way in which issues get framed as a result of the institutional dynamics of the political system.[2] Typically, social-welfare issues are posed as follows: Shall the state undertake to satisfy the social needs of a given constituency and to what degree? Now, this way of framing issues permits only a relatively small number of answers; and it tends to cast debates in quantitative terms. More importantly, it takes for granted the definition of the needs in question, as if that were self-evident and beyond dispute. It therefore occludes the fact that the interpretation of people's needs is itself a political stake, indeed sometimes *the* political stake. Clearly, this way of framing issues poses obstacles for feminist politics, since at the heart of such politics lie questions like, what do various groups of women really need, and whose interpretations of women's needs should be authoritative? Only in terms of a discourse oriented to the *politics of need interpretation*[3] can feminists meaningfully intervene in the coming welfare wars. But this requires a challenge to the dominant policy framework.

Both sets of problems, the structural and the ideological, are extremely important and difficult. In what follows, I shall not offer solutions to either of them. Rather, I want to attempt the much more modest and preliminary task of exploring how they might be thought about in relation to one another. Specifically, I want to propose a framework for enquiry which can shed light on both of them simultaneously.

Consider that, in order to address the structural problem, it will be necessary to clarify the phenomenon of 'public patriarchy.' One type of enquiry which is useful here is the familiar sort of economic analysis alluded to earlier, analysis which shows, for example, that 'workfare' programs function to subsidize employers of low-wage, 'women's work' in the service sector and thus to reproduce the sex-segmented, dual-labor market. Now, important as such enquiry is, it does not tell the whole story, since it leaves out of focus the discursive or ideological dimension of social-welfare programs. By the discursive or ideological dimension, I do not mean anything distinct from or epiphenomenal with respect to welfare practices; I mean, rather, the tacit norms and implicit assumptions which are constitutive of those practices. To get at this dimension requires a meaning-oriented sort of enquiry, one which considers welfare programs as, among other things, institutionalized patterns of interpretation.[4] Such enquiry would make explicit the social meanings embedded within welfare programs, meanings which tend otherwise simply to go without saying.

In spelling out such meanings, the enquiry I am proposing could do two things simultaneously. First, it could tell us something important about the structure of the US welfare system, since it might identify some underlying norms and assumptions which lend a measure of coherence to diverse programs and practices. Second, it could illuminate what I called 'the politics of need interpretation,' since it could expose the processes by which welfare practices construct women and women's needs according to certain specific and in principle contestable interpretations, even as they lend those interpretations an aura of facticity which discourages contestation. Thus, this enquiry could shed light on both the structural and ideological problems identified earlier.

The principal aim of this paper is to provide an account of this sort for the present US social-welfare system. The account is intended to help clarify some key structural aspects of male dominance in welfare-capitalist societies. At the same time, it is meant to point the way to a broader, discourse-oriented focus which can address political conflicts over the interpretation of women's needs.

The paper proceeds from some relatively 'hard', uncontroversial facts about the US social-welfare system (section I) through a series of increasingly interpreted accounts of that system (sections II and III). These culminate (in section IV) in a highly theorized characterization of the welfare system as a 'juridical-administrative-therapeutic state apparatus' (JAT). Finally (in section V) the paper situates that apparatus as one actor among others in a larger and highly contested political field of discourse about needs which also includes the feminist movement.

I

Long before the emergence of welfare-states, governments have defined legally secured arenas of societal action. In so doing, they have at the same time codified corresponding patterns of agency or social roles. Thus, early modern states defined an economic arena and the corresponding role of an economic person capable of entering into contracts. More or less at the same time, they codified the 'private sphere' of the household and the role of household head with dependents. Somewhat later, governments were led to secure a sphere of political participation and the corresponding role of citizen with (limited) political rights. In each of these cases, the original paradigmatic subject of the newly codified social role was male. Only secondarily and much later was it conceded that women, too, could occupy these subject-positions, without however entirely dispelling the association with masculinity.

Matters are different, however, with the contemporary welfare-state. When this type of government defined a new arena of activity — call it 'the social' — and a new societal role, the welfare client, it included women among its original and paradigmatic subjects. Today, in fact, women have become the principal subjects of the welfare state. On the one hand, they comprise the overwhelming majority both of program recipients and of paid social service workers. On the other hand, they are the wives, mothers and daughters whose unpaid activities and obligations are redefined as the welfare state increasingly oversees forms of caregiving. Since this beneficiary–social worker–caregiver nexus of roles is constitutive of the social-welfare arena, one might even call the latter a feminized terrain.

A brief statistical overview confirms women's greater involvement with and dependence on the US social-welfare system. Consider first women's greater dependence as program clients and beneficiaries. In each of the major 'means-tested' programs in the US, women and the children for whom they are responsible now comprise the overwhelming majority of clients. For example, more than 81 per cent of households receiving Aid to Families with Dependent Children (AFDC) are headed by women; more than 60 per cent of families receiving food stamps or Medicaid are headed by women; and 70 per cent of all households in publicly owned or subsidized housing are headed by women (Erie, Rein and Wiget 1983; Nelson 1984). High as they are, these figures actually underestimate the representation of women. As Barbara Nelson (1984) notes, in the androcentric reporting system, households counted as female-headed by definition contain no healthy adult men. But healthy adult women live in most households counted as male-headed. Such women may directly or indirectly receive benefits going to 'male-headed' households, but they are invisible in the statistics, even though they usually do the work of securing and maintaining program eligibility.

Women also predominate in the major US 'age-tested' programs. For example, 61.6 per cent of all adult beneficiaries of Social Security are women; and 64 per cent of those covered by Medicare are women (Erie, Rein and Wiget 1983; Nelson 1984). In sum, because women as a group are significantly poorer than men — indeed they now comprise nearly two-thirds of all US adults below the official poverty line — and because women tend to live longer than men, women depend more on the social-welfare system as clients and beneficiaries.

But this is not the whole story. Women also depend more on the social-welfare system as paid human service workers — a category of employment which includes education and health, as well as social work and services administration. In 1980, 70 per cent of the 17.3 million paid jobs in this sector in the US were held by women. This accounts for one-third of US women's total paid employment and a full 80 per cent of all professional jobs held by women. The figures for women of color are even higher than this average, since 37 per cent of their total paid employment and 82.4 per cent of their professional employment is in this sector (Erie, Rein and Wiget 1983). It is a distinctive feature of the US social-welfare system, as opposed to, say, the British and Scandinavian systems, that only 3 per cent of these jobs are in the form of direct federal government employment. The rest are in state and local government, in the 'private non-profit' sector and in the 'private' sector. But the more decentralized and privatized character of the US system does not make paid welfare workers any less vulnerable in the face of federal program cuts. On the contrary, the level of federal social-welfare spending affects the level of human service employment in *all* sectors. State and local government jobs depend on federal and federally-financed state and local government contracts; and private profit and non-profit jobs depend on federally financed transfer payments to individuals and households for the purchase in the market of services like health care (Erie, Rein and Wiget 1983). Thus, reductions in social spending mean the loss of jobs for women. Moreover, as Barbara Ehrenreich and Frances Fox Piven (1984) note, this loss is not compensated when spending is shifted to the military, since only 0.5 per cent of the entire female paid workforce is employed in work on military contracts. In fact, one study they cite estimates that with each one billion dollar increase in military spending, 9500 jobs are lost to women.

Finally, women are subjects of and to the social-welfare system in their traditional capacity as unpaid caregivers. It is well known that the sexual division of labor assigns women primary responsibility for the care of those who cannot care for themselves. (I leave aside women's traditional obligations to provide personal services to adult males — husbands, fathers, grown sons, lovers — who can very well care for themselves.) Such responsibility includes childcare, of course, but also care for sick and/or elderly relatives, often parents. For example, a 1975 British study cited by Hilary Land (1978) found that three times as many elderly people live with married daughters as with married sons and that those without a close female relative were more likely to be institutionalized, irrespective of degree of infirmity. As unpaid caregivers, then, women are more directly affected than men by the level and character of government social services for children, the sick and the elderly.

As clients, paid human service workers and unpaid caregivers, then, women are the principal subjects of the social-welfare system. It is as if this branch of the state were in effect a 'Bureau of Women's Affairs'.

II

Of course, the welfare system does not deal with women on women's terms. On the contrary, it has its own characteristic ways of interpreting women's needs and positioning women as subjects. In order to understand these, we need to examine how gender norms and meanings are reflected in the structure of the US social-welfare system.

This issue is quite complicated. On the one hand, nearly all US social-welfare programs are officially gender neutral. Yet the system as a whole is a dual or two-tiered one; and it has an unmistakable gender subtext.[5] There is one set of programs oriented to *individuals* and tied to participation in the paid workforce, for example, unemployment insurance and Social Security. These programs are designed to supplement and compensate for the primary market in paid labor power. There is a second set of programs oriented to *households* and tied to combined household income, for example, AFDC, food stamps and Medicaid. These programs are designed to compensate for what are considered to be family failures, generally the absence of a male breadwinner.

What integrates the two sets of programs is a common core of assumptions, underlying both, concerning the sexual division of labor, domestic and non-domestic. It is assumed that families do or should contain one primary breadwinner who is male and one unpaid domestic worker (homemaker and mother) who is female. It is further assumed that when a woman undertakes paid work outside the home this is or should be in order to supplement the male breadwinner's wage and so it neither does nor ought override her primary housewifely and maternal responsibilities. It is assumed, in other words, that society is divided into two separate spheres of home and outside work and that these are women's and men's spheres respectively.[6]

These assumptions are increasingly counterfactual. At present, fewer than 15 per cent of US families conform to the normative ideal of a domicile shared by a husband who is the sole breadwinner, a wife who is a full-time homemaker and their offspring.

Nonetheless, the separate spheres norms determine the structure of the social-welfare system. They determine that it contain a primary labor market-related subsystem and a family- or household-related subsystem. Moreover, they determine that these subsystems be gender-linked, that the primary labor market-related system be implicitly 'masculine' and the family-related system be implicitly 'feminine'. Consequently, the normative, ideal-typical recipient of primary labor market-oriented programs is a (white) male, while the normative, ideal-typical client of household-based programs is a female.

This gender subtext of the US welfare system is confirmed when we take a second look at participation figures. Consider again the figures just cited for the 'feminine' or family-based programs, which I earlier referred to as 'means-tested' programs: more than 81 per cent of households receiving AFDC are female-headed, as are more than 70 per cent of those receiving housing assistance and more than 60 per cent of those receiving Medicaid and food stamps. Now recall that these figures do not compare female vs. male individuals, but rather female vs. male headed *households*. They therefore confirm four things:

1 these programs have a distinctive administrative identity in that their recipients are not individualized but *familialized*;

2 they serve what are considered to be defective families, overwhelmingly families without a male breadwinner;

3 the ideal-typical (adult) client is female; and

4 she makes her claim for benefits on the basis of her status as an unpaid domestic worker, a homemaker and mother, not as a paid worker based in the labor market.

Now contrast this with the case of a typical labor market-based and thus 'masculine' program, namely, unemployment insurance. Here the percentage of female claimants drops to 38 per cent, a figure which contrasts female vs. male *individuals*, as opposed to households. As Diana Pearce (1979) notes, this drop reflects at least two different circumstances. First, and most straightforwardly, it reflects women's lower rate of participation in the paid workforce. Second, it reflects the fact that many women wage-workers are not eligible to participate in this program, for example, paid household service workers, part-time workers, pregnant workers and workers in the 'irregular economy' such as prostitutes, baby-sitters, and home typists. The exclusion of these predominantly female wage-workers testifies to the existence of a gender segmented labor market, divided into 'primary' and 'secondary' employment. It reflects the more general assumption that women's earnings are 'merely supplementary', not on a par with those of the primary (male) breadwinner. Altogether, then, the figures tell us four things about programs like unemployment insurance:

1 they are administered in a way which *individualizes* rather than familializes recipients;

2 they are designed to compensate primary labor market effects, such as the temporary displacement of a primary breadwinner;

3 the ideal-typical recipient is male; and

4 he makes his claim on the basis of his identity as a paid worker, not as an unpaid domestic worker or parent.

One final example will round out the picture. The Social Security system of retirement insurance presents the interesting case of a hermaphrodite or androgyne. I shall soon show that this system has a number of characteristics of 'masculine' programs in virtue of its link to participation in the paid workforce. However, it is also internally dualized and gendered, and thus stands as a microcosm of the entire dual-benefit welfare system. Consider that, while a majority — 61.6 per cent — of adult beneficiaries are female, only somewhat more than half of these — or 33.3 per cent of all recipients — claim benefits on the basis of their own paid work records (Nelson 1984; Erie, Rein and Wiget 1983). The remaining female recipients claim benefits on the basis of their husbands' records, that is, as wives or unpaid domestic workers. By contrast, virtually no male recipients claim benefits as husbands. On the contrary, they claim benefits as paid workers, a labor market-located as opposed to family-located identity. So the Social Security system is hermaphroditic or androgynous; it is internally divided between family-based, 'feminine' benefits, on the one hand, and labor market-based, 'masculine' benefits, on the other hand. Thus, it too gets its structure from gender norms and assumptions.

III

So far, we have established the dualistic structure of the US social-welfare system and the gender subtext of the dualism. Now, we can better tease out the system's implicit norms and tacit assumptions by examining its mode of operation. To see how welfare programs interpret women's needs, we should consider what benefits consist in. To see how programs position women as subjects, we should examine administrative practices. In general, we shall see that the 'masculine' and 'feminine' subsystems are not only separate but also unequal.

Consider that the 'masculine' social-welfare programs are social insurance schemes. They include unemployment insurance, Social Security (retirement insurance), Medicare (age-tested health insurance) and Supplemental Social Security Insurance (disability insurance for those with paid work records). These programs are contributory; wage-workers and their employers pay into trust funds. They are administered on a national basis and benefit levels are uniform across the country. Though bureaucratically organized and administered, they require less, and less demeaning, effort on the part of beneficiaries in qualifying and maintaining eligibility than do 'feminine' programs. They are far less subject to intrusive controls and in most cases lack the dimension of surveillance. They also tend to require less of beneficiaries in the way of benefit-collection efforts, with the notable exception of unemployment insurance. In sum, 'masculine' social insurance schemes position recipients primarily as *rights-bearers*. The beneficiaries of these programs are in the main not stigmatized. Neither administrative practice nor popular discourse constitutes them as 'on the dole'. They are constituted rather as receiving what they deserve, what they, in 'partnership' with their employers, have already paid in for, what they, therefore, have a *right* to. Moreover, these beneficiaries are also positioned as *purchasing consumers*. They receive cash as opposed to 'in-kind' benefits and so are positioned as having 'the liberty to strike the best bargain they can in purchasing services of their choice on the open market'. In sum, these beneficiaries are what C.B. MacPherson (1964) calls 'possessive individuals'. Proprietors of their own persons who have freely contracted to sell their labor-power, they become participants in social insurance schemes and, thence, paying consumers of human services. They therefore qualify as *social citizens* in virtually the fullest sense that term can acquire within the framework of a male-dominated capitalist society.

All this stands in stark contrast to the 'feminine' sector of the US social-welfare system. This sector consists in relief programs, such as AFDC, food stamps, Medicaid and public housing assistance. These programs are not contributory, but are financed out of general tax revenues, usually with one-third of the funds coming from the federal government and two-thirds coming from the states. They are not administered nationally but rather by the states. As a result, benefit levels vary dramatically, though they are everywhere inadequate, deliberately pegged below the official poverty line. The relief programs are notorious for the varieties of administrative humiliation they inflict upon clients. They require considerable work in qualifying and maintaining eligibility; and they have a heavy component of surveillance.

These programs do not in any meaningful sense position their subjects as rights-bearers. Far from being considered as having a right to what they receive, recipients are defined as 'beneficiaries of governmental largesse' or 'clients of public charity'.[7] Moreover, their actual treatment fails to live up even to that definition, since they are treated as 'chiselers', 'deviants' and 'human failures'. In the androcentric-administrative framework, 'welfare mothers' are considered not to work and so are sometimes required, that is to say coerced, to work off their benefits via 'workfare'. They thus become inmates of what Diana Pearce (1979) calls a 'workhouse without walls'. Indeed, the only sense in which the category of rights is relevant to these clients' situation is the somewhat dubious one according to which they are entitled to treatment governed by the standards of formal-bureaucratic procedural rationality. But if that right is construed as protection from administrative caprice, then even it is widely and routinely disregarded.

Moreover, recipients of public relief are generally not positioned as purchasing consumers. A significant portion of their benefits is 'in-kind' and what cash they get comes already carved up and earmarked for specific, administratively designated purposes. These recipients are therefore essentially *clients*, a subject-position which carries far less power and dignity in capitalist societies than does the alternative position of purchaser. In these societies, to be a client in the sense relevant to relief recipients is to be an abject dependent. Indeed, this sense of the term carries connotations of a fall from autonomy, as when we speak, for example, of 'the client-states of empires or superpowers'. As clients, then, recipients of relief are *the negatives of possessive individuals*. Largely excluded from the market, both as workers and as consumers, claiming benefits not as individuals but as members of 'failed' families, these recipients are effectively denied the trappings of social citizenship as the latter is defined within male-dominated capitalist societies.[8]

Clearly, this system creates a double-bind for women raising children without a male breadwinner. By failing to offer them day care, job training, a job that pays a 'family wage' or some combination of these, it constructs them exclusively as mothers. As a consequence, it interprets their needs as maternal needs and their sphere of activity as that of 'the family'. Now, according to the ideology of separate spheres, this should be an honorific social identity. Yet the system does not honor these women. On the contrary, instead of providing them a guaranteed income equivalent to a family wage as a matter of right, it stigmatizes, humiliates and harasses them. In effect, it decrees that these women must be, yet cannot be, normative mothers.

Moreover, the way in which the US social-welfare system interprets 'maternity' and 'the family' is race- and culture-specific. The bias is made plain in Carol Stack's (1974) study, *All Our Kin*. Stack analyzes domestic arrangements of very poor Black welfare recipients in a midwestern city. Where ideologues see the 'disorganization of *the* [sic] black family,' she finds complex, highly organized kinship structures. These include kin-based networks of resource pooling and exchange which enable those in direst poverty to survive economically and communally. The networks organize delayed exchanges or 'gifts,' in Mauss' (1967) sense, of prepared meals, food stamps, cooking, shopping, groceries, furniture, sleeping space, cash (including wages and AFDC allowances), transportation, clothing, childcare, even children. They span several physically distinct households and so transcend the principal administrative category which organizes relief programs. It is significant that Stack took great pains to conceal the identities of her subjects, even going so far as to disguise the identity of their city. The reason, though unstated, is obvious: these people would lose their benefits if program administrators learned that they did not utilize them within the confines and boundaries of a 'household.'

We can summarize the separate and unequal character of the two-tiered, gender-linked, race- and culture-biased US social-welfare system in the following formulae: participants in the 'masculine' subsystem are positioned as *rights-bearing beneficiaries and purchasing consumers of services*. Participants in the 'feminine' subsystem, on the other hand, are positioned as *dependent clients*.

IV

Clearly, the identities and needs which the social-welfare system fashions for its recipients are *interpreted* identities and needs. Moreover, they are highly political interpretations which are in principle subject to dispute. Yet these needs and identities are not always recognized as interpretations. Too often, they simply go without saying and are rendered immune from analysis and critique.

Doubtless one reason for this 'reification effect' is the depth at which gender meanings and norms are embedded in our general culture. But there may also be another reason more specific to the welfare system.

Let me suggest yet another way of analyzing the US social-welfare system, this time as a 'juridical-administrative-therapeutic state apparatus' (JAT).[9] The point is to emphasize a distinctive style of operation. *Qua* JAT, the welfare system works by linking together a series of juridical, administrative and therapeutic procedures. As a consequence, it tends to translate political issues concerning the interpretation of people's needs into legal, administrative and/or therapeutic matters. Thus, the system executes political policy in a way which appears non-political and tends to be depoliticizing.

Consider that, at an abstract level, the subject-positions constructed for beneficiaries of *both* the 'masculine' and the 'feminine' components of the system can be analyzed as combinations of three distinct elements. The first element is a *juridical* one which positions recipients *vis-à-vis* the legal system by according or denying them various *rights*. Thus, the subject of the 'masculine' subsystem has a right to benefits and is protected from some legally sanctioned forms of administrative caprice, while the subject of the 'feminine' subsystem largely lacks rights.

This juridical element is then linked with a second one, an *administrative* element. For in order to qualify to receive benefits, subjects must assume the stance of petitioners with respect to an administrative body; they must petition a bureaucratic institution empowered to decide their claims on the basis of administratively defined criteria. In the 'masculine' subsystem, for example, claimants must prove their 'cases' meet administratively defined criteria of entitlement; in the 'feminine' subsystem, on the other hand, they must prove conformity to administratively defined criteria of need. The enormous qualitative differences between the two sets of procedures notwithstanding, both are variations on the same administrative moment. Both require claimants to translate their experienced situations and life-problems into administerable needs, to present the former as bonafide instances of specified generalized states of affairs which could in principle befall anyone (Habermas 1981).

If and when they qualify, social-welfare claimants get positioned either as purchasing consumers or dependent clients. In either case, their needs are redefined as correlates of bureaucratically administered satisfactions. This means they are quantified, rendered as equivalents of a sum of money (Habermas 1981). Thus, in the 'feminine' subsystem, clients are positioned passively to receive monetarily measured, predefined and prepackaged services; in the 'masculine' subsystem, on the other hand, they receive a specified, predetermined amount of cash.

In both subsystems, then, people's needs are subject to a sort of rewriting operation. Experienced situations and life-problems are translated into administerable needs. And since the latter are not necessarily isomorphic to the former, the possibility of a gap between them arises. This possibility is especially likely in the 'feminine' sub-system. For there, as we saw, clients are constructed as deviant and service provision has the character of normalization — albeit normalization designed more to stigmatize than to 'reform'.

Here, then, is the opening for the third, *therapeutic* moment of the JAT's *modus operandi*. Especially in the 'feminine' subsystem, service provision often includes an implicit or explicit therapeutic or quasi-therapeutic dimension. In AFDC, for example, social workers concern themselves with the 'mental health' aspects of their clients' lives, often construing these in terms of 'character problems'. More explicitly and less moralistically, municipal programs for poor, unmarried, pregnant teenage women include not only pre-natal care, mothering instruction and tutoring or schooling, but also counseling sessions with psychiatric social workers. As observed by Prudence Rains (1971), such sessions are intended to bring girls to acknowledge what are considered to be their true, deep, latent, emotional problems on the assumption that this will enable them to avoid future pregnancies. Ludicrous as this sounds, it is only an extreme example of a more pervasive phenomenon, namely, the tendency of especially 'feminine' social-welfare programs to con-struct gender-political and political-economic problems as individual, psychological problems. In fact, some therapeutic or quasi-therapeutic welfare services can be regarded as second-order services to compen-sate for the debilitating effects of first-order services. In any case, the therapeutic dimension of the US social-welfare system encourages clients to close gaps between their culturally shaped lived experience and their administratively defined situation by bringing the former into line with the latter.

Clearly, this analysis of the US welfare system as a 'juridical-administrative-therapeutic state apparatus' lets us see both subsystems more critically. It suggests that the problem is not only that women are disempowered by the *denial* of social citizenship in the 'feminine' sub-system, although they are. It is also that women and men are disem-powered by the *realization* of an androcentric, possessive individualist form of social citizenship in the 'masculine' subsystem. In both sub-systems, including the 'masculine' one, the JAT positions its subjects in ways which do not empower them. It individualizes them as 'cases' and so militates against collective identification. It imposes monological, administrative definitions of situation and need and so pre-empts dialogically achieved self-definition and self-determination. It positions its subjects as passive client or consumer recipients and not as active co-participants involved in shaping their life-conditions. Lastly, it con-strues experienced discontent with these arrangements as material for adjustment-oriented, usually sexist therapy and not as material for empowering processes of consciousness-raising.

All told, then, the form of social citizenship constructed even in the *best* part of the US social-welfare system is a degraded and depoliticized one. It is a form of passive citizenship in which the state pre-empts the power to define and satisfy people's needs.

This form of passive citizenship arises in part as a result of the JAT's distinctive style of operation. The JAT treats the interpretation of people's needs as pregiven and unproblematic, while itself redefining them as amenable to system-conforming satisfactions. Thus, the JAT shifts attention away from the question: who interprets social needs and how? It tends to substitute the *juridical, administrative and therapeutic management of need satisfaction* for the *politics of need interpretation*. That is, it tends to substitute *monological, administrative processes of need definition* for *dialogical, participatory processes of need interpretation*.[10]

V

Usually, analyses of social complexes as 'institutionalized patterns of interpretation' are implicitly or explicitly functionalist. They purport to show how culturally hegemonic systems of meaning are stabilized and reproduced over time. As a result, such analyses often screen out 'dysfunctional' events like micro- and macropolitical resistances and conflicts. More generally, they tend to obscure the active side of social processes, the ways in which even the most routinized practice of social agents involves the active construction, deconstruction and reconstruction of social meanings. It is no wonder, then, that many feminist scholars have become suspicious of functionalist methodologies; for, when applied to gender issues, these methods occlude female agency and construe women as mere passive victims of male dominance.

In order to avoid any such suggestion here, I want to conclude by situating the foregoing analysis in a broader, non-functionalist perspective. I want to sketch a picture according to which the social-welfare apparatus is one agent among others in a larger and highly contested political arena.

Consider that the ideological (as opposed to economic) effects of the JAT's mode of need interpretation operate within a specific and relatively new societal arena. I call this arena 'the social' in order to mark its non-coincidence with the familiar institutionalized spaces of family and official-economy. As I conceive it, the social is not exactly equivalent to the traditional public sphere of political discourse defined by Juergen Habermas (1975, 1981); nor is it co-extensive with the state. Rather, the social is a site of discourse about people's needs, specifically about those needs which have broken out of the domestic and/or official-economic spheres that earlier contained them as 'private matters'. Thus, the social is a site of discourse about problematical needs, needs which have come to exceed the apparently (but not really) self-regulating domestic and economic institutions of male-dominated, capitalist society.[11]

As the site of this excess, the social is by definition a terrain of contestation. It is a space in which conflicts among rival interpretations of people's needs are played out. 'In' the social, then, one would expect to find a plurality of competing needs discourses. And in fact what we do find here are at least three major kinds:

1 'expert' needs discourses of, for example, social workers and therapists, on the one hand, and welfare administrators, planners and policy makers, on the other;

2 oppositional movement needs discourses of, for example, feminists, lesbians and gays, people of color, workers and welfare clients; and

3 'reprivatization' discourses of constituencies seeking to repatriate newly problematized needs to their former domestic or official-economic enclaves. Such discourses, and others, compete with one another in addressing the fractured social identities of potential adherents.

Seen from this vantage point, the social has a twofold character. It is simultaneously a new arena of state activity and, equally important, a new terrain of wider political contestation. It is both the home turf of the JAT and also a field of struggle which the JAT does not simply control, but on which it acts as one contestant among others.

It would be a mistake, then, to treat the JAT as the undisputed master of the terrain of the social. In fact, much of the growth and activity of the social branch of the state has come in response to the activities of social movements, especially the labor, Black, feminist and Progressive movements. Moreover, as Theda Skocpol (1980) has shown, the social state is not simply a unified, self-possessed political *agent*. It is rather in significant respects a *resultant*, a complex and polyvalent nexus of compromise-formations in which are sedimented the outcomes of past struggles as well as the conditions for present and future ones. In fact, even when the JAT does act as an agent, the results are often unintended. When it takes responsibility for matters previously left to the family and/or economy, it tends to denaturalize those matters and thus risks fostering their further politicization.

In any case, social movements, too, act on the terrain of the social (as do, on a smaller scale, clients who engage the JAT in micropolitical resistances and negotiations). In fact, the JAT's monological, administrative approach to need definition can also be seen as a strategy to contain social movements. Such movements tend, by their very nature, to be dialogic and participatory. They represent the emergent capacities of newly politicized groups to cast off the apparently natural and prepolitical interpretations which enveloped their needs in the official-economy and/or family. In social movements, people come to articulate alternative, politicized interpretations of their needs as they engage in processes of dialogue and collective struggle. Thus, the confrontation of such movements with the JAT on the terrain of the social is a confrontation between *conflicting logics of need definition*.

Feminists, too, then, are actors on the terrain of the social. Indeed, from this perspective, we can distinguish several analytically distinct, but practically intermingled kinds of feminist struggles worth engaging in the coming welfare wars. First, there are struggles to secure the political status of women's needs, that is, to legitimate women's needs as genuine political issues as opposed to 'private' domestic or market matters. Here, feminists would engage especially anti-welfarist defenders of privatization. Second, there are struggles over the interpreted content of women's needs, struggles to challenge the apparently natural, traditional interpretations still enveloping needs only recently sprung from domestic and official-economic enclaves of privacy. Here, feminists would engage all those forces in the culture which perpetuate androcentric and sexist interpretations of women's needs, including, but not only, the social state. Third, there are struggles over the who and how of need interpretation, struggles to empower women to interpret their own needs and to challenge the anti-participatory, monological practices of the welfare system *qua* JAT. Fourth, there are struggles to elaborate and win support for policies based on feminist interpretations of women's needs, policies which avoid both the Scylla of private patriarchy and the Charybdis of public patriarchy.

In all these cases, the focus would be as much on need interpretation as on need satisfaction. And this is as it should be, since any satisfactions we are able to win will be problematic to the degree we fail to fight and win the battle of interpretation.

Notes

I am grateful for the helpful comments, suggestions and criticisms of Sandra Bartky, John Brenkman, Jane Collier, Ann Garry, Virginia Held, Thomas McCarthy, Carole Pateman, Birte Siim, Howard Winant, Terry Winant, Iris Young, and the members of Midwest Society for Women in Philosophy. I also thank Drucilla Cornell and Betty Safford for the invitations which provided occasions for developing the essay; the Stanford Humanities Center for a congenial working environment and financial support; and Dee Marquez and Marina Rosiene for crackerjack word processing.

1 I believe that Brown's terms are too simple on two counts. First, for
   reasons elaborated by Gayle Rubin (1975), I prefer not to use
   'patriarchy' as a generic term for male dominance but rather as the
   designation of a specific historical social formation. Second, Brown's
   public/private contrast oversimplifies the structure of both laissez-faire
   and welfare capitalism, since it posits two major societal zones where
   there are actually four (family, official-economy, state, and sphere of
   public political discourse) and conflates two distinct public-private
   divisions. (For a discussion of this second problem, see Fraser 1985b.)
   These problems notwithstanding, it remains the case that Brown's terms

are immensely suggestive and that we currently have no better terminology. Thus, in what follows I occasionally use 'public patriarchy' for want of an alternative.

2 For an analysis of the dynamics whereby late-capitalist political systems tend to select certain types of interests while excluding others, see Claus Offe (1972, 1974, 1980). For a feminist application of Offe's approach, see Drude Dahlerup (1984).

3 This phrase owes its inspiration to Juergen Habermas (1975).

4 I owe this phrase to Thomas McCarthy (personal communciation).

5 I owe the phrase 'gender subtext' to Dorothy Smith (1984). A number of writers have noticed the two-tiered character of the US social-welfare system. Andrew Hacker (1985) correlates the dualism with class but not with gender. Diana Pearce (1979) and Erie, Rein and Wiget (1983) correlate the dualism with gender and with the dual labor market, itself gender-correlated. Barbara Nelson (1984) correlates the dualism with gender, the dual labor market and the sexual division of paid *and unpaid* labor. My account owes a great deal to all of these writers, especially to Barbara Nelson.

6 Hilary Land (1978) identifies similar assumptions at work in the British social-welfare system. My formulation of them is much indebted to her.

7 I owe these formulations to Virginia Held (personal communication).

8 It should be noted that I am here taking issue with the view of some left theorists that 'decommodification' in the form of in kind social-welfare benefits represents an emancipatory or progressive development. In the context of a two-tiered welfare system like the one described here, this assumption is clearly false, since in kind benefits are qualitatively and quantitatively inferior to the corresponding commodities and since they function to stigmatize those who receive them.

9 This term echoes Louis Althusser's (1984) term, 'ideological state apparatus'. Certainly, the US social-welfare system as described in the present section of this paper counts as an 'ISA' in Althusser's sense. However, I prefer the term 'juridical-administrative-therapeutic state apparatus' as more concrete and descriptive of the specific ways in which welfare programs produce and reproduce ideology. In general, then, a JAT can be understood as a subclass of an ISA. On the other hand, Althusserian-like terminology aside, readers will find that the account in this section owes more to Michel Foucault (1979) and Juergen Habermas (1981) than to Althusser. Of course, neither Habermas nor Foucault is sensitive to the gendered character of social-welfare programs. For a critique of Habermas in this respect, see Fraser (1985b). For my views about Foucault, see Fraser (1981, 1983 and 1985a).

10 These formulations owe much to Juergen Habermas (1975, 1981).

11 I borrow the term 'social' from Hannah Arendt (1958). However, my use of it differs from hers in several important ways. First, Arendt and I both understand the social as an historically emergent societal space specific to modernity. And we both understand the emergence of the social as tending to undercut or blur an earlier, more distinct separation of public and private spheres. But she treats the emergence of the social

as a fall or lapse and she valorizes the earlier separation of public and private as a preferred state of affairs appropriate to 'the human condition'. I, on the other hand, make no assumptions about the human condition; nor do I regret the passing of the private/public separation; nor do I consider the emergence of the social a fall or lapse. Secondly, Arendt and I agree that one salient, defining feature of the social is the emergence of heretofore 'private' needs into public view. But Arendt treats this as a violation of the proper order of things. She assumes that needs are wholly natural and are forever doomed to be things of brute compulsion. Thus, she supposes needs can have no genuinely political dimension and that their emergence from the private sphere into the social spells the death of authentic politics. I, on the other hand, assume that needs are irreducibly interpretive and that need interpretations are in principle contestable. It follows from my view that the emergence of needs from the 'private' into the social is a generally positive development since such needs thereby lose their illusory aura of naturalness, while their interpretations become subject to critique and contestation. I, therefore, suppose that this represents the (possible) flourishing of politics, rather than the (necessary) death of politics. Finally, Arendt assumes that the emergence of the social and of public concern with needs necessarily means the triumph of administration and instrumental reason. I, on the other hand, assume that instrumental reason represents only one possible way of defining and addressing social needs; and that administration represents only one possible way of institutionalizing the social. Thus, I would argue for the existence of another possibility: an alternative socialist-feminist, dialogical mode of need interpretation and a participatory-democratic institutionalization of the social.

References

Althusser, L. (1984), 'Ideology and Ideological State Apparatuses: Notes towards an Investigation'. In Althusser, *Essays on Ideology*. London: Verso.

Arendt, H. (1958), *The Human Condition*. Chicago and London: The University of Chicago Press.

Barrett, N.S. (1984), 'The Welfare Trap'. Unpublished manuscript.

Brown, C. (1981), 'Mothers, Fathers, and Children: From Private to Public Patriarchy'. In *Women and Revolution*. L. Sargent, ed. Boston: South End Press.

Dahlerup, D. (1984), 'Overcoming the Barriers: An Approach to the Study of How Women's Issues are Kept from the Political Agenda'. In *Women's Views of the Political World of Men*. J.H. Stiehm, ed. Dobbs Ferry, NY: Transnational Publishers.

Ehrenreich, B. and Fox Piven, F. (1984), 'The Feminization of Poverty'. *Dissent*. Spring 1984: 162–70.

Erie, S.T., Rein, M. and Wiget, B. (1983), 'Women and the Reagan Revolution: Thermidor for the Social Welfare Economy'. In *Families, Politics, and Public Policies: A Feminist Dialogue on Women and the State*. I. Diamond, ed. New York and London: Longman.

Foucault, M. (1979), *Discipline and Punish: The Birth of the Prison*. Alan Sheridan, tr. New York: Vintage.

Fraser, N. (1981), 'Foucault on Modern Power: Empirical Insights and Normative Confusions'. *Praxis International* 1:272–87.

—— (1983), 'Foucault's Body-Language: A Post-Humanist Political Rhetoric?' *Salmagundi* 61:55–70.

—— (1985a) 'Michel Foucault: A "Young Conservative"?' *Ethics* 96:165–84.

—— (1985b) 'What's Critical About Critical Theory? The Case of Habermas and Gender'. *New German Critique* 35:97–131.

Habermas, J. (1975), *Legitimation Crisis*. Boston: Beacon.

—— (1981), *Theorie des kommunikativen Handelns*, Band II, *Zur Kritik der funktionalistischen Vernunft*. Frankfurt am Main: Suhrkamp Verlag.

Hacker, A. (1985), ' "Welfare": The Future of an Illusion'. *New York Review of Books*. February 28, 1985:37–43.

Land, Hilary (1978), 'Who Cares for the Family?' *Journal of Social Policy* 7:257–84.

MacPherson, C.B. (1964), *The Political Theory of Possessive Individualism: Hobbes to Locke*. New York and London: Oxford University Press.

Mauss, Marcel (1967), *The Gift: Forms and Functions of Exchange in Archaic Societies*. I. Cunnison, tr. New York and London: W.W. Norton & Company.

Nelson, Barbara J. (1984), 'Women's Poverty and Women's Citizenship: Some Political Consequences of Economic Marginality'. *Signs: Journal of Women in Culture and Society* 10:209–31.

O'Connor, J. (1973), *The Fiscal Crisis of the State*. New York: St Martin's Press.

Offe, C. (1972), 'Political Authority and Class Structure: An Analysis of Late Capitalist Societies'. *International Journal of Sociology* 2:73–108.

—— (1974), 'Structural Problems of the Capitalist State: Class Rule and the Political System. On the Selectiveness of Political Institutions'. In *German Political Studies*. Klaus von Beyme, ed. London: Sage Publications.

—— (1980), 'The Separation of Form and Content in Liberal Democratic Politics'. *Studies in Political Economy* 3:5–16.

Pearce, D. (1979), 'Women, Work, and Welfare: The Feminization of Poverty'. In *Working Women and Families*. Karen Wolk Feinstein, ed. Beverly Hills, CA: Sage Publications.

Rains, P.M. (1971), *Becoming an Unwed Mother: A Sociological Account*. Chicago: Aldine Atherton, Inc.

Rubin, G. (1975), 'The Traffic in Women: Notes on the "Political Economy" of Sex'. In *Towards an Anthropology of Women*. R.R. Reiter, ed. New York: Monthly Review Press.

Skocpol, T. (1980), 'Political Response to Capitalist Crisis: Neo-Marxist Theories of the State and the Case of the New Deal'. *Politics and Society* 10:155–201.

Smith, D. (1984), 'The Gender Subtext of Power'. Unpublished manuscript.

Stack, C.B. (1974), *All Our Kin: Strategies for Survival in a Black Community*. New York, Evanston, San Francisco, London: Harper & Row.

Chapter eight

Socialism as a Sociological Problem

Irving Velody

It is both attractive and plausible to accept Marx's view that only within the possibilities of nineteenth-century thought and the social conditions which give rise to that intellectual process, does socialism appear as a viable undertaking: one, indeed, which may take on the form and reality of an effective social organization and reorganization.

It is plausible, too, to see that sociology with its general investment in accounting for all aspects of social phenomena, must also concern itself with the nature of socialism. This concern must encompass the character of socialism as a belief system, socialism's own claim to be a form of knowledge and finally, and most significantly for the direction of sociology itself, the political vision of socialism and the relation of that vision to sociology's own claims to comprehend the political axis of human behaviour.

While this sociological interest in socialism has been long established, what appears to have been neglected is the extent to which both undertakings share a range of suppressed premises; and that with this intellectual communism they share, too, in a series of unresolved and possibly unresolveable problems.

I

[the essence of thought, this order] . . . must rather be of the purest crystal. But this crystal does not appear as an abstraction, but as something concrete, indeed as the most concrete, as it were the hardest thing there is. (Wittgenstein: *Philosophical Investigations*, §97)

In pursuing the solution to a problem it is often easier to attend to investigations in another realm of knowledge. Occasionally a singular element is extracted, brought under close examination, and willingly or otherwise, is exposed to that intellectual piracy which so characterizes the human sciences; and amongst those sciences none more so than sociology and its cognates which have captured, encompassed, absorbed or revised paradigms, Darwinism, psychoanalysis, and whole linguistic theories — to mention only the merest fragment of such a list.

In the present case art history provides a short cut and a remarkably economic procedure for dealing with the problem under discussion. This is not to say that art history differs significantly in its mimetic potential from other human sciences. Apart from the standard pattern of a triumphalist progression linked to a transcendental essential copy (see below), the genre abounds in marxian analysis; psychohistory; applications of Piagetian genetic epistemology entwined with Kuhnian paradigms (Gablik 1977); and semiotics (Iversen 1986). However, these innovations remain, to a surprising extent, interwoven with features of the standard pattern.

In *Vision and Painting*, Norman Bryson brilliantly adumbrates one specific concept: The Essential Copy. I can do no better than to repeat Bryson's quotation from Dante with all it implies:

> Once Cimabue was thought to hold the field
> In painting; now it is Giotto's turn;
> The other's fame lies buried in the dust.

Cimabue had found again the (lost) perceptions of the artists of antiquity: that ability to paint, that is to report in painting on the reality of the natural world. Cimabue's work is as much involved in discovery as in 'art', assuming that such a distinction might hold. And with that opening to the world there followed Giotto whose researches and achievements were to surpass Cimabue within this dimension of the natural. As Bryson puts it, Vasari in *Lives of the Artists* was to expand this tale 'into a whole saga of triumph and obsolescence, beginning with . . . Cimabue and Giotto and culminating in Michelangelo, hero, genius . . .'

Of course there have been other such discoveries and rediscoveries in painting, most notably with regard to perspective. In spite of Panofsky's monograph, *Perspective as Symbolic Form*, the question of perspective remains unresolved as to whether it is indeed a scientific discovery or a cultural invention. But rather similar questions arise as to the discoveries of sociology as we shall see.

It is time to look at the major features of the doctrine of the Essential Copy. These may be summed up under three aspects:

1 The image is thought of as self effacing entity . . . The goal towards which it moves is the perfect replication of a reality found existing 'out there' already . . .

2 Each advance in art consists of the removal of a further obstacle between painting and the Essential Copy.

3 All men are agreed that Giotto's registration of the visual field is subtler, etc., and in every way superior to that of Cimabue. Thus advance and progress in painting is open to recognition and general agreement. The criterion for this is of course fidelity to the Essential Copy. (Bryson 1983: 6–7)

While this is not the place to consider the adequacy or otherwise of Bryson's formulations of historiographical practice in art history, it should be noted that his work does not stand alone. More recently Hans Belting has surveyed a range of similar issues (1987; and also Danto 1987). In any case what is striking about these accounts (and Bryson's in particular) is their proximity, in terms of style and objective, to the 'research methodologies' of both sociology and socialism.

For what lies behind this doctrine are two major themes brought inseparably together. The most obvious undercurrent is the dynamic of painterly achievement; in a parallel to the developmental account of science, we learn of how the registration of perceptions on the canvas accrues increasing sophistication and verisimilitude. A kind of Popperian progress of knowledge is in view. Over time, through the ages, western artists have grasped the true aspects of the object; emerging from the confusion and muddle of Medieval versions of reality, with their stylized images of the body and their strange displays of space and volume, by degrees the real image begins to emerge. Underlying the initial perception exists this piece of reality awaiting its full depiction. Again we may be put in mind of Popper's critical rationalism. Perhaps certain (artistic) experiments have taken a wrong turning; have entered a cul-de-sac. But the potential for learning and testing painterly techniques remains an ever-present goal. And in considering the diachrony of painting we see how the base or substratum of the Essential Copy presides over artistic achievement guiding the artist in the attempt to reproduce the real world. Within the historical process lies the extra-temporal reality effectively awaiting discovery. It is in this sense that perspective may be seen as a discovery.

That this approach is not peculiar to painting can be seen from Watkin's illuminating study of architecture and its historians, and particularly his account of Nikolaus Pevsner, where he writes:

> [Pevsner's interpretation] asserted that art must express the essence of a still unborn society struggling to realise the potentiality of a socialistic industrial technology overlain by the dying remains of Victorian capitalism. The new architecture was to be integral . . . to the 'idea' of a socialist industrialism that had yet to be realised.
>
> (Watkin 1977)

In his comment on Pevsner, 'The underlying principle remains the same throughout Pevsner's work: art must "fit" into the *Zeitgeist* which is now a progressive harbinger of the earthly New Jerusalem', Watkin appears to detect the symptoms and operations of the Essential Copy at work.

Clearly these characteristics of the Essential Copy must be found outside of specific historical episodes. The object is a continent awaiting its explorer, possessing a transcendental quality with regard to merely human visions and cultural illusions.

This progressive, forward-moving account of art history thus requires its transcendental object. It would be difficult to make sense of the claim to progress if this claim did not imply some kind of *telos*; here the *telos* is the Essential Copy. Thus the diachrony of this type of historiography is encoded with its synchrony; the theme of progress chained to the transcendental object.

II

We are under the illusion that what is peculiar, profound,
essential in our investigation resides in trying to grasp the incom-
parable essence of language. That is, the order existing between
the concepts of proposition, word . . . and so on. This order is a
super-order — between so to to speak — super–concepts.

(Wittgenstein: *PI*, §97)

The purpose of this section is two-fold: to characterize certain salient features of sociological analysis, particularly those types of theories that have been especially influential in assessing the nature of socialism, and to consider the consequences of these formulae and their problems. But while the focus is on systemic, general theories of society such as those deriving from Marx and Durkheim or more latterly Talcott Parsons, some of the technical issues may be applied to a much wider range of theories, including those based in some way on concepts of the agent or subject.

There are at least two major themes in systemic theories which mirror Bryson's account of the Essential Copy. The clearest aspect appears in the diachronic project expressed by writers such as Marx and Durkheim. Quite consistently the analyst proffers a view of social change and social structure: the transitions from the simpler pre-industrial relationships of mechanical solidarity to the complex processes indicated within organic, industrial society. Or with Engels' 'all successive historical systems are only transitory stages in the endless course of human society from the lower to the higher' (1946). Certainly, wherever such theorists concern themselves with the nature of knowledge and changes in its con-stitution, all are constrained to recognize science and its cognate activities as both itself advancing and in some necessary sense a component of more general advances in society at large.

However, while triumphalist versions of history are widely recog-nized in the literature, what is less analysed is the nature of the underly-ing theoretical dimension relating to the imagery of society which such theories provide. A study of the apparatus proffered by such mainstream theory (as I shall term it from now on) brings to light a number of specific features.

Perhaps the most significant of these is the assumption of an interior mechanism concealed beneath a (relatively) superficial integument. 'If there were no difference between essence and appearance there would be no need of science' (Marx). Compare this to Durkheim's methodological prescriptions: 'the determining cause of a social fact must be sought among antecedent social facts and not among the states of the individual consciousness'. Further, 'The primary origin of any social process of any importance must be considered in the *internal* constitution of the social environment' (Durkheim 1938; my emphasis). Finally, consider Talcott Parsons' Kantian view of sociological theory as made up of a set of theoretical propositions standing in logical interrelation to each other so that they constitute a logically closed system (1949). Such theories are in agreement that immediate empirical evidence is quite insufficient to provide an adequate explanation of social phenomena. Further, mainstream sociology requires that explanation of the phenomena or happenings must be adduced to a mechanism which gives rise to such surface phenomena. Precisely what these mechanisms are and how they are linked to the observational data is a matter of dispute. But that such mechanisms are linked, and connected causally to empirical features of the world, is not at issue.

It does not seem too contentious to sustain this as an account of mainstream sociology. However, whether or not theorists pay much attention to their own epistemological claims, that is whether they clearly comprehend their procedural requirements in terms of adequate foundations for their knowledge of the social, it is certainly true that the bulk of academic production in this field reflects issues of method, even if at a fairly trivial level. To put it slightly differently, epistemology is rapidly transformed into methodology. Expressions of anomie, alienation, modernization and so on, may be measured and the conditioning variables, unavailable to immediate observation, may thus be estimated. What is of moment here is the concealment of a series of problems that operate within the heartland of theorizing, certain lacunae that appear in the linkage between the central generative mechanism concealed within the recesses of society and the imputed processes that, ultimately, produce the surface phenomena which are all that are available for observation.

We may take mainstream sociology then to be making a series of claims about the nature of knowledge; its relation to social processes; the kinds of explanation required to account for these processes; and the role of the analyst and the form of the technical language employed. To put the matter briefly this tradition assumes social phenomena to require both interpretation and causal explanation. For to speak of social phenomena here is to claim that what actors, agents, say or do is not what these actions and doings really signify. These significations lie elsewhere, very much in the heart of society, and indeed are finally determined by causal mechanisms, the beating heart which both orders society and moves it through time.

In a sense these forces and the order they sustain constitute the essential copy of sociology. That we have in this account a highly abstract image, a reality which is certainly not immediately available to the observer, makes it no less powerful an instrument. The pressure of constraining norms or the determining effects of the social relations of production, or the strength of rationalization, all these factors are no less real merely because the actor does not see them. In a strange kind of way they are more real, real, say, in the way a natural scientist might confirm natural effects invisible to the eye of the layman (for instance ultra-violet radiation).

Just precisely why this model of explanation has been so widely adapted cannot be discussed here, although investigation of the Enlightenment movement has been indicative of the pattern. However, of the many problems that arise in the sociological project I want here to note two: the relation of cause and meaning and the relation between the language of the observer and the speech of the actor.

The first of these shows itself in all structural or systemic accounts of society; the discourse of actors is a product of a mechanism or process sited elsewhere in the social process. Durkheim's social facts are only the beginning of analysis; they are themselves the product of other forces. Rigorous analysis demands that such phenomena as acts of suicide, or the actor's expression of belief or truth, are functions of a specific apparatus. The view that there are forces, say at the level of the social relations of production, powerful enough to causally determine the content of the actor's discourse is not unique to sociology. It is a standard manifestation in psychology and a particularly interesting feature of Freud's account of human action and the subject's self-reportage on experience.

This area has received extensive attention in the philosophy of the social sciences, although the conclusions drawn are largely ignored by practitioners. To put the matter briefly, all arguments that assert that actors' statements are functions of underlying (not-intentional) mechanisms, which are generally claimed to be causal in nature, rest on a misunderstanding about the nature of explanation. The major point here is that statements of an intentional kind, those statements where agents give reasons for their actions, cannot be translated or redescribed in terms of a new set of statements which replace intentions with causes. This being the case all claims to being able to account for 'ideologies', or more generally 'belief systems', in so far as accounts here stand for a causally effective determining apparatus or something like it, lack all cogency and must be regarded as without validity or coherence.

The second aspect, the problem of the relation between two kinds of language or discourse, raises more extensive difficulties. The view that the analyst must develop a more accurate form of dealing with social events of course runs parallel with the general conception of knowledge and its constitution. This conceives of a well-founded discipline as one which sustains itself by a form and structure that lies within or beneath appearance: here, specifically, those appearances which provide the major source of data for the human sciences, spoken or written utterances produced or emitted by the subject.

The attempt to establish a firm foundational structure for the human sciences initially appears to be no more than an analogue to the natural science programme of the development of a perspicuous language for handling its own data. However, unlike the natural sciences, this programme inevitably creates a problem, or at the very least raises a question about the relation between the language of the analyst and the cultural products (including the expressions of its subjects) of society.

This kind of problem has a venerable lineage in the philosophy of science. It is perhaps no coincidence that the programme of the Vienna Circle was centrally concerned with the development of just such a high level language which could provide the foundation for *all* science, namely the project of a unified science. Although Logical Empiricism was a most influential movement its goals were never fulfilled. It is worth noting Wittgenstein's early contact with this group, as in many ways *Philosophical Investigations* can be seen as a response to claims to have access to a special, more powerful language than vernacular forms can provide.

For sociology there are, then, three significant themes which emerge from the programme for the establishment of a privileged language: first, the elimination of difficult-to-handle actors' formulations — often by the translation of those expressions entailing the reasons-for-acting formulae into some non-intentional type of terminology; secondly, the adoption of the doctrine that significant language terms represent states of affairs, and are in some sense pictures of reality; and finally, the claim to a formal structure of language which is free of everyday practices and can represent the complex causal mechanisms behind society through the application of suitable observational data.

The characteristics of such formal languages might look something as follows: a scientific (or social scientific) language might have the following *desiderata*: that it be essentially extensional, its lexicon basically referential or constituted by logical operations; that its structure is coherent and makes some kind of syntactical sense; certainly that it can be considered itself to be a system which operates, analytically at least, independently of other systems (such as a social system); and that such a language should have universal application. This semiotic should have the ultimate virtue of being prior to, or having epistemological priority to, ordinary talk and chat. Such languages are more accurate and make more transparent the relations of social phenomena to theoretical entities.

This discussion of powerful language theories, examples of which could well refer to such as those derived from Chomsky, de Saussure, or the Vienna Circle, in itself mirrors many of the earlier claims about the Essential Copy. In this case the claim is that behind the cloudy verbal interactions of ordinary folk exists a powerful systematically organized force, language, the deep grammar of which appears but fragmentarily in its surface manifestations; or as an alternative formulation, that the background *langue* is carried about unwittingly in the heads of actors who seemingly converse in low level *parole*.

It has been very much the consequence of Wittgenstein's investigations to reveal the central incoherence of such a programme. For Wittgenstein, language as an activity becomes conceptually incoherent when displayed as an autonomous region outside of the practical activities of human subjects. In this approach the problem is that there is nowhere else to go to observe language; there is no exterior point beyond the realm of concrete language practice. Special languages may give the appearance of greater power, and for certain (limited) purposes they can be put to work. But they are entirely dependent for their own meanings and significations on the operations of everyday discourse. Parsons' search for a foundational 'analytic realism' is thus a doomed quest; its Kantian overtones will not save appearances.

Again, if this critique is true, the structure, indeed the very rationale of the sociological programmes of explanation through generative mechanisms via powerful technical languages, is totally invalidated. Whatever the findings of writers like Durkheim, Marx or Parsons may mean, their significance cannot be accepted on the basis of the investigator's own programme.

To return to the general discussion, standard accounts of sociology require a generative mechanism to explain surface events; and this mechanism is in a sense transcendental, outside and beyond short-term changes in the empirical. This apparatus bears interesting comparison with Bryson's Essential Copy. Both structures account for a particular product (painting, society) and both provide a template against which the state of society (or painting) can be assessed. Conditions of acute anomie or major class conflict are indicative of an instability or lack of order. Yet the logic of the underlying theory implicitly commands such orderliness if social life is to continue at all. The formal structures of social theories carry with them a satisfying symmetry which may be at odds with surface appearances. But ultimately, if society is even to survive, it must conform to these deeper imperatives commanded by these generative mechanisms. The reality of society is to be found at this level, not within the terms of expression of the subjects of society. The Essential Copy generates the data which provides the possibility of an accurate representation of reality. Just as the adequacy of painting may thus be judged in these terms, so the adequacy of society may be assessed by its capacity to abide by the deep grammar which operates within.

III

Thought is surrounded by a halo. — Its essence, logic, presents an order, in fact the a priori order of the world: that is the order of possibilities which must be common to both world and thought. But this order . . . is prior to all experience, must run through all experience; no empirical cloudiness or uncertainty may be permitted to affect it —

(Wittgenstein: *PI*, §97)

If Berki is right in his comment that the state should be seen as a contestable social concept, it must be no less true that this characteristic applies to the generality of terms applied in the discernment of social institutions. But the consequence of this view is not recognized as an inherent difficulty in explaining social processes. Rather it becomes an occasion to circumvent such matters by prescribing a clear-cut apparatus which will, if only in the 'last instance', give rise to those cloudy states of affairs, everyday social reality.

This indeed has been the strategy embedded in the major lines of descent flowing from Marx and Durkheim. While disagreeing with many doctrinal details of these thinkers it has been the task of later commentators essentially to revise and reformulate accounts of the social world in terms that expand the plausibility of the explanatory mechanisms in these contexts. Yet this has been a paradoxical undertaking for the work of Max Weber.

Weber's commentary on socialism — in contrast to Marx and Durkheim — seems to contain a strange mixture of warnings about feasibility, threats of bureaucratization and ethical opposition to certain ends. But what is not on offer is a contrasting alternative world; and in this respect Weber is far from the accounts of Marx and Durkheim. We seem to be reading a *feuilleton* rather than a scientific report. As Mommsen puts it, 'For Weber there were no objective laws of social reality . . . Weber's radical position followed unavoidably from the fundamental premise that history is meaningless in itself' (Mommsen 1985).

Yet the 'weakness' of Weber's analytic strategy is generally put to one side. Rather, interpreters have profiled the theme of rationality, to discover as it were yet another mechanism of social production and reproduction which will distantly mirror those other discoveries owed to Durkheim and Marx. For Schluchter, as well as Bendix, Weber formulates a process of rationality and rationalization incorporating both a dynamic and synchronic dimension of social order and change. In temporal terms world history, or more cautiously European history, demonstrates the working out, admittedly in a very complex way, of the power of substantive and institutionalized rationality; the major features of this process can be discerned in the rise of western science;

the development of a rationally organized system of production and accounting; the evolution of ratio-legal administrative rules; and the necessary domination of bureaucratic organizations within these societies. The synchronic aspect of this process can again be recognized in the major features of social organization and its economy; its scientism, its rationalistic forms of social relationships — again through bureaucratization. The general picture afforded by these features would not of themselves suggest much difference between the view of Marx and Weber; or indeed Hegel, who might stand as the major suppressed premise in western social science. In its scientific guise, Socialism, whatever the status of its ethical ideals, is conceived of as the effective working out of rationality (as a grounded process, rather than an aethereal ideal) in all aspects of social affairs. The functions of many, possibly all, social institutions under such perspicuous and substantive rational activities — that is the life of mankind under true socialism — become redundant. If the class basis of the state is swept away its necessity ceases to be; institutions sustained by law, legitimacy based on violence, marriage and private property, again would have no functional component. If science is universally accessible, and if indeed a true social science is installed, the distinction between appearance and reality will end. And with it will end social science itself. The matter at issue here is not one of the utopian nature of such a world; but more a concern with the consequences of an underlying syntax and logic, by and through which the world is to be grasped.

It is quite impossible to read Weber as offering such a programme at any level of analysis. His comments on methodology stress the constant possibility of social innovation and of the revision of research programmes. Again for Weber the analysis of cultural artefacts and meanings do not afford explanation through general laws. The value-relevance (or value-relationship) of the observer forecloses on such an eventuality; for the social world may be sectioned for investigation in an illimitable number of ways. No essential copy lies in wait for the social investigator to discover; there are, quite simply, no such discoveries to be made.

Since Weber affords so minimal a grasp of inner social processes can his stance be taken as a foundation for sociology? Talcott Parsons had no doubts about the severe limitations in Weber's work when noting as a problem how Weber seemed to be concerned merely with the shuffling around of ideal types (Parsons 1949).

It is less surprising then that for the present discussion two major features may be engaged in Weber which appear to be absent in the mainstream sociological tradition: first, the omission of any clear account of central generative forces, an account which the community of scholars might assess at the level of causative mechanisms in terms of explaining the appearance of the surface phenomena of the social, in short, the lack of a penetrating explanation of social phenomena in history and society.

Rather, we are presented with the work of a *bricoleur* . . . and this is perhaps Parsons' real complaint.

More positively, Weber does offer us an account, indeed a whole range of analyses, of the polity. And here his position is very much opposed to that theme in sociology which subsumes politics as, in some sense, within and beneath other, more general regulative processes; again Parsons' own views do not differ substantially in their logic from Marx and Durkheim.

Weber's contrast with the mainstream tradition is striking. In *Socialism* Durkheim writes '[Socialism] . . . is not a scientific formulation of social facts, it is itself a social fact . . . an object of science' (1962). LaCapra's discussion clarifies the implications:

> Corporatism . . . would make socialism more than a bread and butter issue. It would respond to the socialist 'aspiration for a rearrangement of the social structure by relocating the industrial set-up in the totality of the social organism, drawing it out of the shadow where it was functioning automatically, summoning it into the light and the control of the conscience' . . . Through corporatism the social question would become 'not a question of money or force', but a 'question of moral agents'.
>
> (LaCapra 1972)

There is no great methodological distance from Marx's, 'When the proletariat announces the dissolution of the existing social order it only declares the secret of its own existence.' This point can be expanded with Engels' statements that '[With] these two great discoveries, the materialistic conception of history and the revelation of the secret of capitalistic production through surplus value . . . Socialism became a science' (1970). That is, the special cognitive tools of scientific socialism reveal the inner nature of society. And further 'In modern history . . . the state — the political order — is the subordinate, and civil society — the realm of economic relations — the decisive element' (1946). It follows that with the existence of a society where relationships are transparent, so to speak, then it makes sense to say as Cohen does 'Marx's view of science in socialism is that it is redundant' (1978).

That this procedure is current practice can be seen from some varieties of feminist social theory. In this case a concept like 'patriarchy' can be unpacked and put to work to provide causal explanations for (unequal) social relationships. The conjunction of theoretical model with moral imperatives demonstrates the ease with which political action and programme may be inscribed in a social analysis. While definitional terms may differ, the logic of explanation and analysis is isomorphic with the standard pattern.

What then of the function of politics in these two schemata, socialism and sociology? For both, the nature of the realm of political activity requires it to play a subordinate, not to say ephemeral role. The rearrangement of social relations is the essence of the political. Failure to carry out these refashionings must entail a flawed society, no matter what claims can be made within the field of political doctrine or activity. The application of valid social knowledge is the precondition of the effective society. Sociology and socialism must both unmask the character of society; it is in this sense that both undertakings share a common goal and a unitary methodology.

IV

> Someone says with every sign of bewilderment . . . 'I do not know there is fog on the road unless it is accompanied by an illuminated sign saying "fog".'
>
> (Frayn: *Fog-like Sensations*)

If the cognitive structure of socialism mirrors that of sociology it follows that they will either contest the same terrain, or merge. It has of course been the argument of this paper that this is precisely the case. As socialism requires a causally adequate analysis of social affairs it, too, as a cognitive system, rests upon the same kinds of foundations as sociology.

For socialism, as a political activity, as a grounded praxis, the particular paradoxical curiosity of this is the conception of politics as epiphenomenal when considered in relation to those central generative forces which give rise to society.

It follows at once that if the general critique of mainstream social science is correct then these same problems apply to socialism. It is the subversion of these cognitive foundations, the erosion of the methodological programme of the human sciences as extended from the Enlightenment, that Rorty and Lyotard have seen as the end of the grand metanarratives and thus as the moment of the postmodern.

Of the many interesting problems that arise from this discussion one in particular calls for some comment, although no definitive solution can be promised. Essentially this appears as a question: given the developing critiques that appear in the debate over the bases and metaphysics of the human sciences, do not these reassessments themselves indicate the transition to a new social and historical era; or at the very least point to the existence of a radically novel intellectual landscape? In short have we reached the plateau of postmodernity?

The principal protagonists of this debate, Habermas, Rorty and Lyotard, seem to agree on one thing at least: either that something really new has happened — and then application of the key term has some cogency (Lyotard, Rorty); or, effectively, there is merely the appearance of novelty, but essentially we are concerned with a continuation of previous themes, perhaps no more than the question of the latest intellectual fashion (Habermas, Merquior).

As an avowed child of the Enlightenment, for Habermas this much is clear: philosophy, and by this we may read Habermas as speaking of a philosophical anthropology, is still possible and has the aim of 'clarifying the possibilities of processes of reaching understanding, which may be presumed to be universal in that they are necessary'. Although this is a round about way of stating things this position seems exceedingly close to admitting essentialist claims to special forms of knowing and returns us to the standard foundationalist package.

Rorty has clearly recognized these problems in Habermas. In response to Habermas' indictment of postmodernist thought as neo-conservative, Rorty writes that in operating with a conception of 'postmodernist bourgeois liberalism' he holds to a political usage free of the Kantian buttresses of transcultural and ahistorical accounts of morality and rationality. The term 'postmodernist' is taken in the sense given by Lyotard: the postmodern attitude is that of distrust of metanarratives (Rorty 1983). However, before falling to the temptations of the new order it is well to consider what procedural moves are involved in the postmodern. If postmodernity is conceived as another step, or stage, we have again returned to the processual development established in standard chronologies of social change. And if, apparently more humbly, we regard it as merely a symptom of a deeper condition, again we are reclaiming the discredited programme of the hidden mechanism as our mentor. One sympathizes with Merquior's observation that postmodernism is still largely a sequel to, rather than a denial of, modernism (1986).

In spite of the conceptual problems that inhabit the undertakings of our grand narratives, socialism and sociology, and despite the empirical 'disconfirmations' in both provinces, there is no reason to expect either activity to disappear in the foreseeable future. Discussions like Alex Nove's point to the practical difficulties involved in the execution of socialist economic programmes (1983). And John Dunn has stressed the consequences of socialism's epiphenomenal view of politics as the problem of finding superior alternatives to

> the patient struggle to transform capitalist democracies for the better through their constitutionally sanctioned political institutions. It is still an open question . . . how far such transformation can go *benignly* in a socialist direction.
>
> (Dunn 1984; my emphasis)

Yet, just as mainstream sociology will continue to generate its products and papers in spite of highly damaging theoretical assessments and in the face of constant empirical rebuffs, socialism itself as a central part of the world that gave birth to the human sciences, as part of the goal of the comprehension of humanity's condition and the release from its enslavement to ignorance and cultural (mis-)arrangements, will continue as well.

Note

I have not attempted to outline the varieties of socialist thought and practice which in any case would be an impossible task. I have attempted to show the epistemological links with social science, although presenting this latter undertaking in a particular way, simply because this version of sociology makes strong and clear statements about the character of the world. The omission of actor-oriented theories should not be taken as an implicit acceptance of such social theories. On the contrary phenomenological and hermeneutically based versions of social behaviour mirror the problems of the generative mechanisms discussed above. The kind of difficulties that an Husserlian based social theory (such as that of Alfred Schutz) may encounter have been well brought out by Derrida (1973); and a sensitive report on the presumptions at work in Charles Taylor's political hermeneutics can be consulted in Shapiro (1986). Quotations from *The Rules of Sociological Method* are from Margaret Thompson's translation in Thompson (1985). Finally thanks must go to my colleagues Harriet Bradley and Peter Lassman for their invariably helpful comments and suggestions.

References

Belting, H. (1987) *The End of the History of Art?* Chicago: University of Chicago Press.

Berki, R.N. (1988) 'Vocabularies of the State', this volume.

Bryson, N. (1983) *Vision and Painting*, London: Macmillan.

Cohen, G.A. (1978) *Karl Marx's Theory of History: A Defence*, Oxford: Oxford University Press.

Danto, A.C. (1987) 'Interruptions to Progress', *Times Literary Supplement*. Sept 18–24; 1015.

Derrida, J. (1973) *Speech and Phenomenona*, Evanston: Northwestern University Press.

Dunn, J. (1984) *The Politics of Socialism*, Cambridge: Cambridge University Press.

Durkheim, E. (1938) *The Rules of Sociological Method*, Chicago: University of Chicago.

—— (1962) *Socialism*, New York: Collier.

Engels, F. (1946) *Ludwig Feuerbach and the End of Classical German Philosophy*, Moscow: Progress Publishers.

—— (1970) *Socialism: Utopian and Scientific*. Moscow: Progress Publishers.

Gablik, S. (1977) *Progress in Art*, New York: Rizzoli.

Iversen, M. (1986) 'Saussure v. Peirce: Models for a Semiotics of Visual Art'. In A.L. Rees and F. Borzello (eds) *The New Art History* London: Camden Press.

LaCapra, D. (1972) *Emile Durkheim*, Ithaca: Cornell University Press.

Lyotard, J.-F. (1984) *The Post-Modern Condition: A Report on Knowledge*, Manchester: Manchester University Press.

Merquior, J.G. (1986) 'Spider and Bee: A Critique of the Postmodern Ideology', in *Postmodernism, ICA Documents 4 & 5*. London: Institute of Contemporary Arts.

Mommsen, W.J. (1985) 'Capitalism and Socialism: Weber's Dialogue with Marx', in R.J. Antonio and R.M. Glassman (eds) *A Weber–Marx Dialogue*. Lawrence: University of Kansas Press; 234–261.

Nove, A. (1983) *The Economics of Feasible Socialism*, London: Allen & Unwin.

Panofsky, E. (1975) *La perspective comme forme symbolique*, Paris: Minuit.

Parsons, T. (1949) *The Structure of Social Action*, New York: The Free Press.

Rorty, R. (1983) 'Postmodernist Bourgeois Liberalism', *Journal of Philosophy* 80 (10):583–9.

—— (1985) 'Habermas and Lyotard on Postmodernity', in Richard Bernstein (ed) *Habermas and Modernity*, Cambridge: Polity Press, 161–75.

Schluchter, W. (1981), *The Rise of Western Rationalism: Max Weber's Developmental History*, Berkeley: University of California Press.

Shapiro, M.J. (1986) 'Charles Taylor's Moral Subject', *Political Theory* 14 (2):311–24.

Thompson, K. (1985) *Readings from Emile Durkheim*, London: Ellis Horwood/Tavistock.

Watkin, D. (1977) *Morality and Architecture*, Oxford: Oxford University Press.

Weber, M. (1971) 'Socialism', in J.E.T. Eldridge (ed) *Max Weber: The Interpretation of Social Reality*, London: Michael Joseph; 190–219.

Wittgenstein, L. (1967) *Philosophical Investigations*, Oxford: Blackwell.

Chapter nine

Postmodernity and Contemporary Social Thought

Wayne Hudson

Post-philosophy is difficult terrain. The prospects for intellectual history are also not good — unless it is possible to develop contemporary historical consciousness as an active engagement, radically recuperative in its relation to the unsaturated past, but also deftly concerned with contemporary political and social issues. The effective interface between post-philosophy and contemporary intellectual history is yet to be achieved. In its absence, old fashioned virtues of clarity and coherence deserve a rerun. This paper is an attempt to begin the task of tidying up a particularly confused part of the contemporary intellectual landscape.

The current international discussion of postmodernity is characterized by confusion and conceptual slippage. Different accounts of postmodernity are advanced by different authors, accounts which fail in most cases to clearly observe the differences between:

1 the modern–postmodern distinction;
2 the modernism–postmodernism distinction;
3 the modernity–postmodernity distinction.

Over and over again books and articles appear in which 'postmodern' is confused with 'postmodernist' and 'postmodernism' is confused with 'postmodernity'. Account after account conflates:

1 postmodernity as an alleged new era or epoch after the modern;
2 postmodernity as an alleged phase of modernism or after modernism;
3 postmodernity as a new philosophical climate.

Many writers assume that the case for 1 is strengthend by the existence of 2 and 3, even though 3 is indebted to 2, an ageing phenomenon which essentially predates the scientific and technological determinants of our emerging global situation.

I

What is postmodernity? The call for definition is classical but contemporary. Talk of postmodernity has become the mode in tertiary

institutions as well as among advertizers, artists, architects, cultural pro-
moters generally. This makes for distrust. Obviously it is important to
remain clear headed when faced with the advertizing hype of capitalist
entrepreneurship not least when such hype characterizes the aspirant
outpourings of the academy. The firmness of the fashion is deceptive.
No satisfactory account of postmodernity yet exists, although
archaeologies of postmodernity are well under way in German.

Prima facie postmodernity may be characterized as the 'post' of
whatever 'modernity' is taken to be. This solution turns out to be
problematic since modernity is used in divergent senses, not all of which
permit of a 'post', and because temporal succession is not decisive for
all accounts of postmodernity. Further, the exact relation between
'modernity' and 'postmodernity' is controverted. Thus postmodernity
may be dubbed: the belatedness of modernity (*Nachtraglichkeit*), the last
phase of modernity, a radicalization of modernity, a retreat from
modernity, the transcendence of modernity, a dialectical crisis of modernity, a critique of modernity — to give only a sample of the available
possibilities.

Other uncertainties also pertain. The attempt to undermine modernity by declaring it to be 'dead', 'over' or 'superseded' is not new.
Catholic writers such as Romano Guardini and Eugene Rosenstock-
Huessey were announcing 'the overtaking' of modernity and *das Ende
der Neuzeit* between the wars. However, the generality of the contemporary perception that modernity has aged and the widespread enthusiasm
for taking leave of it announce something else. But this something else
may not be postmodernity. Even if a consensus were to emerge that
'modernity' is now belated, this would not necessarily involve a transition from modernity to postmodernity in a substantive sense. We could
live through the end of modernity without arriving at postmodernity.

Nor is the precise relation between postmodernity and modernization immediately obvious. Postmodernity is widely interpreted as an
over-reaction to the pathological consequences of capitalist modernization. However, postmodernity may also be interpreted as more modernization, as more:
differentiation
secularization
rationalization
reflexivity
freedom
choice
autonomy
disenchantment
fragmentation

There are also difficulties associated with the expectation that
postmodernity will involve a significant *change* of some sort. This may

be no more than recognition of the commodity status which cultural change has acquired in capitalist countries. The notion that postmodernity is new is also contested. Postmodernity is sometimes regarded as *a restoration* (of tradition, of memory after modernist forgetting) or *a counter-reformation* or *a resurgence* of out of date ideologies and attitudes, or as *a rebirth* or *a repetition* for example of mannerism or the baroque.

Consistent with these difficulties, postmodernity is currently characterized in the international literature in inconsistent and even contradictory ways. Specifically, it is characterized (*inter alia*) as:

1 a myth
2 periodization
3 a condition or situation
4 an experience
5 an historical consciousness
6 a sensibility
7 a climate
8 a crisis
9 an episteme
10 a discourse
11 a poetics
12 a retreat
13 a topos
14 a task or project

1 Postmodernity as a Myth

Postmodernity may be characterized as a myth. This account relies on rejecting the identifications for postmodernity proposed, and on attacking the alleged element of prophecy involved in talk of postmodernity. Such considerations tend to be falsely sophisticated. Like arguments against the existence of Santa Claus, they are half-enlightened. Naturalistically conceived, the problem is to determine whether or not postmodernity exists or whether there are adequate reasons for expecting that it will come in time to do so. Given this stance, it is possible to dismiss claims that postmodernity exists already, or will come to exist in time, as no more than voluntaristic *prophecy*. This objection however is less sophisticated than it first sounds. The anticipatory character of such proclamation is not necessarily suspect. As Kumar showed in *Prophecy and Progress* (1978), the industrial revolution was theorized *before* it happened. But the naturalist approach towards the existence or non-existence, the coming or non-coming of postmodernity itself needs to be questioned. Our accounts of postmodernity may themselves constitute a situation rather than represent a situation external to them. They may be coercive and formative. They may even be self-fulfilling.

Postmodernity is not a myth in the sense of a falsehood. It is a myth in the sense of a piece of chronopolitical bric-à-bric, but then this is all it *could be*. Hence, the charge that postmodernity is a myth needs to be reformulated.

2 Postmodernity as a Periodization

Postmodernity may be *a periodizing term* or *a periodization*. Those who take postmodernity as a periodizing term appear unable to agree on when postmodernity begins. Thus 'postmodernity' is alleged to have begun 100 years ago and only 25 years ago; to be just beginning and to be still to come; to be now; to be something recently gone; to be a recurrent structural possibility reappearing in determinate periods.

This account has considerable force as a register of felt changes but little or no standing as nomenclature. We may well be in a periodizing space which needs a label. To this extent the term 'postmodernity' can be used to register the alleged fact that we live in an intravenient space at the end of the modern age. Postmodernity may also be used to mean postmodern times, the postmodern era, age or epoch which has either already begun or is about to come. But this usage is too indeterminate to gain wide acceptance. It is also arbitrary and involves a confusion of modern with modernity. It is *the modern era* which is reaching its close on this account. Postmodernity might designate the ending up phase in which modernity as one aspect of the modern era also declines. It can hardly designate the new age or epoch which follows the modern.

3 Postmodernity as a Situation

Postmodernity may be characterized as *a situation or condition*. But *what* situation or condition, and *where* is it alleged that this situation or condition can be found? In so far as a particular and possibly unique condition is alleged to pertain, reference may be made to:
a the organization of knowledge and research;
b consciousness and sensibility;
c values;
d culture;
e the organization of work and leisure;
f patterns of settlement.

On this account postmodernity may be glossed in terms of alleged changes in society and economy. For example: in terms of the alleged coming of 'post-industrial' society. The idea that contemporary society was assuming a new technologically determined form was a prominent theme in the writings of Marshall McLuhan (*Understanding Media*, 1964) and in the speculations of Buckminister Fuller, even before Amitai Etzioni called postwar society 'postmodern' in *The Active Society* (1965).

Nonetheless, the existence and alleged characteristics of such a 'post-industrial society' remain disputed. Many of the alleged transitions have either not occurred or have proven transitory, for example the shift from goods to services, the emergence of white collar dominance. Others dismiss the concept of post-industrial society as a form of capitalist ideology which encourages the illusion that capitalism has changed fundamentally and that class struggle no longer takes place. On this view claims about the decline of work and talk of information as the new 'capital' (cf. Bahro, Gorz, Galtung, Toffler) are simply dangerous. A more historical objection denies that industrial society itself ever existed and so refuses the term 'post-industrial' altogether.

Alternatively, postmodernity may be glossed in terms of the coming of the computer age, the age of advanced technology, the information age, the media age, the age of instant communications. This account draws heavily on cybernetics, systems theory and communication theory models. It implies that fundamental transformations of society are brought about by changes in the organization of knowledge and technology without reference to political and social struggles. On this account, it is the post-traditional developments, made possible by advanced technology and science, which need to be discussed. The emergence from traditional human life and society which made modernity necessary is carried further.

Those who posit a new cultural situation or condition often appeal to *postmodern culture*: as a post-traditional culture, as a culture of cannibalism, as a detranscendentalized self-referential culture, as a culture of nihilism, as a *post*-culture. Alternatively, postmodernity can also be dubbed a revolution in the way in which our culture thinks of itself: a revolution which calls into question the dominant values of the last four centuries. In some discussions related to developments in the media and influenced by Baudrillard, postmodernity may be high talk for the allegedly schizophrenic culture of 'late capitalism'. This account emphasizes alleged negative consequences of capitalist modernization: the destruction of the past, the erosion of traditional culture, the decline of bourgeois values, the demoralization of society, the implosive effects of electronic media, the kitsch world of para-aesthetic stimuli.

Postmodernity may then be theorized as the arrival of nihilism: a state in which the highest values of western civilization finally devalue themselves, a condition in which the finalities of modern western culture have collapsed. On this account what is in issue is a post-historical rather than postmodern condition: a condition in which the intelligibilities of western historical experience are subverted, in which traditional meanings and values are destroyed, in which referentiality fails and all finalities appear suspect and exhausted.

Postmodernity, however, may also be characterized more systematically by reference to an alleged reorganization of knowledges and related changes in social organization and institutional structure. Here the work of Lyotard is of exceptional interest. The problem is that many such assertions about the reorganization of knowledges turn out to be armchair extrapolations or generalizations of local and shortlived trends. That such reorganizations of knowledges are occurring may be true, but if they are, it is far from certain that such reorganizations will have the character alleged by writers on postmodernity. Further, the detail required to establish that 'modernity' is the relevant relation and 'post' the modifier, may be conspicuously absent both before and after the relevant research is done. In short, this usage involves prospection purporting to be reportage or description.

4 Postmodernity as an Experience

Postmodernity may also be characterized as *an experience* or as a set of modes of experiencing. It may be alleged that a new experience (for instance of historical time) has emerged, or that a set of new modes of experiencing already follow in the wake of new media or new technology. Alternatively, the new modes of experiencing in question may be still to come. This account parallels the accounts of modernity developed by Baudelaire and Simmel. It is subject to the same difficulties:

a that the experiences alleged may be incapable of serving as candidates for individuation since they apply to only some regions of the phenomena under study; and

b that they combine affirmative stances towards such changes with alleged phenomenologies of them.

5 Postmodernity as an Historical Consciousness

Postmodernity may be characterized as *an historical consciousness*. Here the outstanding insight is that new chronopolitical spaces, new horizons of expectation, may be becoming available to human beings. Nonetheless, such an account is difficult to make out in detail. No doubt there is a new stance towards modernity in the air. Thus a recursive referential stance is sometimes recommended as the precondition for the next major advance. Just as the Renaissance involved a new model of narrative time and a valorization of innovation, so postmodernity might involve a new interpretation of history defined by its stance towards modern times (*Neuzeit*) rather than antiquity. Alternatively, postmodernity may also be associated with *post-histoire*: the end of history topos proclaimed in France by Kojève and continued by contemporary French Nietzscheans such as Deleuze. A time of laughter and transgression when the dead live, an end game.

Or, yet again, postmodernity may be associated with a problematizing of linear history in the name of multi-temporality, polyphony and discontinuities. It may be possible to draw a parallel between this questioning of the normativity of linear periodization and the Renaissance's need to interpret itself as a rebirth of classical antiquity. But the implication of the parallel is subversive. For on this account those who come after the moderns in time will not want to be postmoderns. They will deny the reference and dispute the genealogy.

6 Postmodernity as a Sensibility

Postmodernity can also be characterized as *a sensibility* or syndrome. This sensibility can be characterized as:

a a non-totalizing sensibility which refuses traditional unifications and homogenizations;

b a sensibility which desires complexity and rejoices in antinomian play;

c a sensibility which is accepting of disorder, discrepancies, discontinuities and gaps, which delights in paradoxes and contradictions, and which is prepared to countenance and make allowance for the unpresentable;

d a sensibility which refuses a new equilibrium;

e a sensibility which respects difference and heterogeneity, which is attentive to the singular and the particular rather than the abstract generic, a sensibility which marks out and reverences incommensurable qualities between different areas of life, different cultures and centuries, different psychologies and genders.

On this account postmodernity is a matter of new ethical attitudes rather than of specific cultural trends which may prove short lived. What is at stake is a refusal of coercion, compulsion, terror, violence. This account is of exceptional interest, especially in so far as it specifies modernity in terms of violent or heteronomous unifications and totalizations — of the self, of society, of the work of art. It is subject to the difficulty that such unifications and totalizations may not properly relate to modernity. They may be older. Similarly, the real problems involved in such unifications may not yield to the simple moralism evident in much writing influenced by Levinas or Foucault. Violence may be non-defeasible. On the other hand, the increased sensibility to the repression of 'difference' and heterogeneity, or, in the case of women, to the virtual non-representation of half of humanity, can only be regarded as a major advance. Modernity and postmodernity, however, may be the wrong terms in which to theorize this advance.

7 Postmodernity as a Climate

Postmodernity may be characterized as *a climate* or a temper: a climate of ideas, attitudes, values. This account is often firmed up by more precise specification in terms of *alleged changes in philosophical stances*. Many such stances can be linked with attempts to break with liberal humanism and the individualism central to it. Here the Althusserian notion that such humanism is the 'ideology' of 'bourgeois society' runs with more technical convictions that certain theses about the production of meaning, consciousness and the subject have been shown to be mistaken. Characteristically confusion prevails between the claim that certain doctrines have been advanced by contributors to French Critical Theory, and the claim that those doctrines have been made out or established. Nonetheless, there are frequent references to:

a the end of humanism and the death of the subject, or, in later versions, the de-centring of 'man' or the subject;
b the end of representation;
c the end of realism or mimesis;
d the end of truth, or the contemporary inability to distinguish between truth and falsehood, appearance and reality;
e the need to recognize our unavoidable immanence (in language, society, history, the body), the lack of any transcendent standpoint, the impossibility of a transcendental signifier;
f the centrality of interpretation, understood as inherently political, linguistically shaped, rhetorical, contestable and incomplete;
g a new understanding of mathematics as derived from language and of logic as derivative from metaphor and rhetoric;
h the reorientation of contemporary criticism to the tropes of discourses.

Major shifts are alleged away from realism, objectivism and epistemological transcendence towards immanentism, historicism, conventionalism, constructivism and fictionalism. In strong versions not only humanism, but rationalism, empiricism and representation are regarded as exploded fables. The 'humanist' ideology of transparent representation and immediate experience is exposed as false. It is simply taken for granted that culture is inherently a field of contested codes and representations, and that science is not above history or independent of the politics of language. Given the Nietzschean coloration and the stress on interpretation which invents rather than represents its object, much is made of relativity, discontinuity, paradox, the aleatory.

All this is exciting, if over-dense. Nonetheless, there is a consistent misuse of terminology involved as post-structuralist discussions are labelled 'postmodernism', despite their obvious modernist inspiration and the modernist commitments of many of the key theorists, and this alleged postmodernism is then mislabelled postmodernity or alleged, without clear criteria, to bring in postmodernity in its wake. The double confusing of post-structuralism with postmodernism, and postmodernism with postmodernity, makes rational analyses of the associated claims unnecessarily circuitous.

Another problem is that those accounts of postmodernity which emphasize new philosophical stances, ideas, values or attitudes often fail to relate these to actual changes in the world. Indeed radical versions of the former often justify passivity towards the latter. Those who identify postmodernity with post-structuralism for example are either silent or vague about the new technology. A reference to computer terminals or to electronic media is hardly sustained treatment.

8 Postmodernity as Crisis

Postmodernity may also be characterized in terms of *a crisis*. For example, as a crisis of authority in (and of) Western European culture: a crisis of values, of legitimation, of finalities. At the most general level this crisis may be detailed in Lyotard's terms as a crisis of the metanarratives (*meta-récits*) allegedly characteristic of modernity or even of western culture since the Renaissance. Postmodernity on this account involves the detranscendentalization and delegitimation of western culture. The possibility of any overarching metaheory or meta-discourse is rejected, and this rejection is widely taken to be characteristically 'postmodernist', although the grounds for such rejection tend to be garbled pluralism, Nietzschean revivalism, and neo-Wittgensteinian talk of incommensurable 'language games'.

Or yet again postmodernity may be characterized as *an aesthetic* crisis: as a crisis of traditional aesthetic criteria and doctrines as cultural productions appear which fail to fall within the provenance of such doctrines. Here postmodernity is a misnomer for postmodernism, where postmodernism itself is a misnomer for a wide diversity of post-traditionalist, allegedly anti-aesthetic tendencies.

Alternatively the crisis may be construed as *a crisis of the Enlightenment*. Contemporary criticism of the Enlightenment questions the benefits of an unqualified rationalism and argues that such rationalism has had harmful or disintegrating effects, and has led to a more refined oppression rather than to emancipation. The Enlightenment utopias of emergence from myth and liberation from illusion are questioned. Progress, equality and human perfectibility are seen as naive totalizations. This development may be expressly linked to the dialectic of enlightenment theorized by Adorno and Horkheimer: to the process by which reason becomes destructive, nihilistic, cynical and destroys all the legitimations which enlightened reason put in the place of myth. Postmodernity then becomes the nihilistic conclusion or outcome of modernity.

9 Postmodernity as an Episteme

Postmodernity may also be characterized as *an episteme*. There may be

references, for example, to a postmodern episteme characterized in terms
of:
a epistemological scepticism;
b antirationalism;
c antinomianism;
d pluralism;
e immanence;
f relativity;
g indeterminacy;
h discontinuity and disjunction;
i acceptance of chance, the aleatory, disorder;
j incommensurability.
But such talk is inflationary. No appropriate criteria for identifying *an
episteme* are given. Even if they were, such an account would be too
strong for the label 'postmodernity'. Much more than modernity would
be superseded, just as aspects of modernity could be continued.

10 Postmodernity as a Discourse

Postmodernity may be characterized as *a discourse*: postmodernist
discourse. Postmodernist discourse turns out to mean the theoretical
discourse of structuralist and post-structuralist French critical theory,
above all discourse about the subject, the body, desire, and language.
On this account Lacan, Deleuze, Guattari and Lyotard become key
figures. But the use of 'discourse' here is improper and it is nowhere
established that such a discourse exists. Further, even if a change of
discourse were to be established, it would not be clear why 'modernity'
would be the appropriate entity to be 'posted' by such a development.
The discourses of modernity might change, without them being replaced
by a single discourse called postmodernity.

11 Postmodernity as a Poetics

Postmodernity may also be characterized as *a poetics*. Alternatively,
organizational changes in the nature of aesthetics or of art objects may
be alleged. Or, yet again, new relations between the reader and the text,
and between the current inter-text and other inter-texts or con-texts, may
be alleged. However, there is really no reason to use the term 'postmodernity' here, except to maintain the parallel with the mistaken use
of modernity as a pseudo-nominalization for modernism.

12 Postmodernity as a Retreat

Postmodernity is also characterized as *a retreat*: a retreat from the project of enlightenment or the project of modernity. On this account postmodernity is associated with the rejection of the ideals of the Enlightenment: its universalism, its belief in equality and in progress, its goal of the realization of reason in history. Postmodernity is said to be a retreat from the project of modernity in the sense of the project of realizing reason in history and/or the project of achieving a future rational and humane society. Alternatively, postmodernity is associated with a rejection of Marxism and of the dialectic, teleology, philosophy of history and totality central to it. However, the term 'retreat' is desperately prejudicial and requires precisely the kind of fake teleology under attack.

The same holds for attempts to take postmodernity to be cultural decline, the decay of something, a falling away, i.e. *belated* modernism.

13 Postmodernity as a Topos

Postmodernity may be characterized as *a topos*: as a cultural space in terms of which large parts of contemporary culture are discussed and re-evaluated. This account has the advantage of highlighting the productivity of postmodernity as a theme regardless of the final judgement on it as cultural nomenclature. Thus, it is clearly the case that postmodernity as a topos can be related to *a search for new stances in many of the main departments of contemporary culture*. Specifically, it can be related to quests for new stances towards:
humanism
rationality
history
legitimation
imagination
mythology
science
technology
religion
Of course, postmodernity as nomenclature is likely to disappear in so far as the discussion of such topics results in the emergence of something else — unless reasons can be found for elongating the period of transition.

14 Postmodernity as a Project

Finally, postmodernity may be characterized as *a project or task*. This account accommodates any failure of postmodernity to appear. There is no agreement, however, as to what postmodernity as a project or task would be. On one account postmodernity as a project or task would be the attempt to rethink the democratic universalism of the Enlightenment, individual and collective self determination, and the goal of realizing reason in history in pluralist non-totalizing terms. But it might also be argued that postmodernity could be the task of continuing or reviewing modernity by resisting the concessions to pluralism the earlier account implies. Once again, there is no strong ground for the label 'post-modernity', except a possible parallel with talk of the project of modernity.

II

What are the implications of all this for contemporary social thought? Here I concentrate on four groupings: 1 topological implictions; 2 revisionary implications; 3 implications which go to the mode of discourse; 4 implications which go to social location.

Topological Implications

Postmodernity as a topos has implications for contemporary social thought which go beyond the cultural contents so far projected onto it. Such filler should not prejudice disillusioned observers against *the site*. The diverse accounts of postmodernity distinguished in Section I can serve to accelerate cultural clearance. No doubt these diverse characterizations of postmodernity have a certain objectivity insofar as they represent different entry points into the discussion and specific regional locations: linguistic, geographic, disciplinary, artistic, political. They also have a certain analytical value. Once these accounts of postmodernity are differentiated, they can be used to tidy up the chronic confusion in the international discussion of postmodernity. Many participants will then be found to conflate distinct accounts of postmodernity and to slide from one account to another in a methodologically uncontrolled manner. Nonetheless, the plurality of these accounts, and their tenuous basis in many cases, must give rise to concern.

It will not do to attempt to reconcile these accounts on the grounds that postmodernity is an essentially contested concept for which family resemblances between diverse accounts are all that can reasonably be expected (Palmer, 1985:11). Postmodernity is not *a concept* at all. Further, the confusion and disorder which these diverse accounts reflect are not accidental or without significance. They point to objective *impedimenta* in the way of a rational engagement with our contemporary world. These *impedimenta* include a continuing tendency to view matters from a recursive standpoint and to fail to project an adequate long-term future horizon. They also include an inability to grasp our own causal role as historical actors without falling into voluntarist delusions, a pervasive will to secure 'reality' and 'truth' in a domain from which we ourselves and our comportments are excluded.

This occlusion of our own activity gives many of the controversies

about postmodernity an objectivistic character which in turn renders them spurious. To get beyond the abstract oppositions of the current literature it is useful to distinguish between two different questions:
1 does the state of affairs alleged or implied by a particular account of postmodernity in fact pertain?
2 is this state of affairs well labelled 'postmodernity'?
It is important not to centre on the second question too quickly. In historical nomenclature generally the names employed by the actors tend to be promotional, inaccurate and misleading, shaped by considerations of advantage or context rather than by purely analytical considerations. Indeed, there is a need for actors not to be held back by considerations appropriate to scholarly redescription, as if those who want to assert a trend should be expected to get its dimensions correct *unterwegs* or to provide in advance the end points which are the prizes in the struggle. Hence the frequent need for later scholarship to draw the distinctions differently.

In the case of 'postmodernity' operational and analytical nomenclature are frequently confused, despite the fact that the power bids first to have postmodernity, and, more recently, to be rid of it, are discernible now, whereas the best analytical cutting of the phenomena involved may not be evident for decades. An historically sophisticated approach therefore needs to take both considerations into account without coming to premature judgements.

Above all, the appearance of new topological possibilities needs to be highlighted and not concealed by an excessive concentration on the prevalence of hype and self promotional cultural inflation. Here the tiresome 'post' may be double coded. It is not merely that postmodernity can be regarded *pari passu* with post-industrial, post-Marxist, post-history and post-capitalism — all doubtful. Rather the point is that the *post* may be more important than first identifications of what it is the post of. References to a 'post' may be more important than the residue term to which they are affixed. Thus post-*culture* or post-*industrial* may not have much force, but some of the key features alleged may deserve fore-grounding. The most important accounts of postmodernity may be those for which the label is least justified. Again, postmodernity might be *a preferred nominalization*, even if the grounds for such a nominalization do not exist — just as another nominalization may be chosen for what analytically may be dubbed postmodernity. Art history abounds in such phenomena.

What is new topologically is a spacing after the modern: a spacing which begins empty and attracts unsuccessful attempts to fill it. Once this is recognized the implication arises for contemporary social thought that chronopolitical self-thematization is unavoidable, always provoked and constrained, but ultimately unfoundable. Seen in the context of humanity's partial freedom, the issue then becomes how to weight the merits of various *self-thematizations*, granted that the merits of such thematizations cannot in principle be reduced to anteriorities. Instead, our own action in making up historical typing needs to be acknowledged. Similarly, the chronopolitics of such historical typing needs to be frankly exposed and acknowledged so that the merits of projecting this or that socio-historical imaginary (Castoriadis) can be made the subject of rational argument, without pretending that rationality itself can make the key choices for us. Our farewell to the security of the recursive view may be gradual, but the long-term significance of any dawning willingness to take our own chronopolitical actions seriously and to subject them to rational reflexivity could be considerable. Even if postmodernity as constructed thus far is *a manifestation of our cultural backwardness vis-à-vis the problems which confront us*, a site has been found from which to signal our emergence from traditional anteriorities and the possibility of a further maturation of our reflexivity whereby we learn to accept responsibility for our chronopolitical projections and historical comportments.

Revisionary Implications

The revisionary implications of the current international discussion of postmodernity will take decades to work through in rigorous terms. Here I outline only four.

One major revisionary implication of the international discussion of postmodernity for contemporary social thought is *the need to problematize the notion of 'modernity' itself*: to expose its totalizations, unifications and evasions, to question the endemic bias in modernity's favour without lapsing into modish or intellectually irresponsible anti-modernity. In this context it would be helpful to revalue the most important critiques of modernity, including:

1 the Hellenic critique of modernity which emphasizes the occlusion of classical distinctions in modernity and the fall into historicist voluntarisms;
2 the gnostic critique of modernity which emphasizes the negative consequences of the mundanization or disenchantment of the world, the decline of noetic, the loss of a qualitative and objectively heterogeneous cosmos, the vulgarization of everyday life, the substitution of fictions for imaginal contents. Here the works of R. Guénon, F. Schuon, Henri Corbin and S. Nasr deserve attention;
3 the traditionalist Catholic critique of modernity, which emphasizes the anti-intellectualist character of modern life, its irrational cult of subjective experience and intuition, its unprincipled historicism, materialism and social atomism, the loss of an organic approach to work, the modern domination of nature;

4 the Islamic critique of modernity, which focuses on modernity's secularism, its dehumanization, its lack of genuine community, its alleged degradation of women;

5 the sociological critique of modernity, according to which modernity rests on an illusory cult of potentially autonomous individuals who will be able to realize this autonomy if only they are liberated from repressive social institutions and allowed unconstrained freedom to choose for themselves on an *ad hoc* basis. This critique emphasizes the harmful effects of attempts to break out of all social parenting. It advocates an end to attempts to release individuals from any matrix of social accountability and for a return to covenant responsibility and to the systematic nurturing of multi-generational traditions and institutions;

6 the marxist critique of modernity (found, for example, in Henri Le Febvre) for which modernity accomplishes some of the aims of the revolution, but in a distorted and fragmentary way. According to this critique, modernity achieves the critique of bourgeois life and carries alienation to extremes, but it fails to make possible the appropriation by man of his own nature or the transformation of everyday life;

7 the Heideggerian critique of modernity which emphasizes its subjectivism, its forgetfulness of Being, its will to power which manifests as destructive technology.

Such critiques may be refunctioned to spell out many of the pathologies of modernity, including the pervasive nihilism, triviality and disloyalty of modern social life, the inability to deal with death, the lack of integration with the universe, the absence of a narratable community. They can also alert us to the chauvinism which operates in existing discussions of modernity and call into question the chauvinism of the modern/pre-modern distinction in particular. In so far as such chauvinism is called into question, it is likely that major terminological revisions will be mandatory. In so far as a discussion of postmodernity leads us to appreciate the chauvinism of the modern/pre-modern distinction, this appreciation may strike at the modernity/postmodernity distinction as well. Hence, by an indirect route, the current discussion of postmodernity may end in *a rejection of its own terms of reference*. In so far as the need for more rigorous terminology is admitted, the term 'modernity' is likely to be found wanting. Postmodernity may not fare any better. It is not necessary to accept the existence of postmodernity in order to appreciate that contemporary technoscience is providing the contours of a different world. Postmodernity may be obsolete chauvinist nomenclature which falls away as the object comes into clearer view.

A second revisionary implication of the discussion of postmodernity is *the need to open up the whole question of whether it is possible to refunction, reconstellate or even supersede entirely the sphere divisions of modern culture*. The Weber–Habermas attempt to ground such differentiation of spheres in the anteriority of a process of rationalization must be questioned — and not only from a standpoint which regards such differentiation as contingent, the outcome of specific relations of power and administrative controls.

A third revisionary implication concerns the *contemporary status of rationality and the need to re-evaluate the leading themes and historical role of the European Enlightenment*. This implication is discussed with considerable verve by both Lyotard and Wellmer (Lyotard, 1984; Wellmer, 1983, 1985).

In its most striking version it is suggested that the 'totalizing' thought of modernity, its 'totalized' subject, its 'totalized' reason, its 'totalized' social unity and its 'totalized' aesthetic production can all now be overcome and replaced by more open and pluralistic alternatives. Similarly, western culture can be detranscendentalized: its transcendental pretensions, abstract univcrsality and need for legitimations, foundations and grounds can all be overcome. But the issues raised are immensely complex and require more careful work on the social history of thought than is yet available. At the very least the implication is that contemporary social thought needs to explore ways in which modern notions of rationality can be problematized and related to specific social histories, ways in which a more pluralistic approach to rationality might be constructed, even multiple aporetically-related rationalities. One certain outcome will be that contemporary interpretations of the problem ('totalized', 'transcendental') will turn out to be over-fast, even-superficial.

A fourth revisionary implication concerns *the need to rethink attempts to found social thought on an overarching 'theory'*. This in turn requires a re-evaluation of the status of 'theory' in different contexts and a clarification of the different kinds of theory needed in each. In the process it will become clear that the attempt to have theory found our social thought is a piece of residual anteriority which it is becoming possible to do without. *Once we recognize explicitly that in many practical contexts theory is not what we primarily need, a different constellation of social thought becomes visible.* This needs to be spelt out in detail elsewhere. Clearly there is need for caution. A rejection of an overarching theory could have undesirable side effects. It could favour certain forms of political and religious irrationalism. This itself however alerts us to the need to recognize that *the problem of irrationalism is unsolved in western societies and requires sustained contemporary attention.* A social thought which handled 'theory' in another way would need to be able to show that it could limit and enclave irrationalism successfully. It would also need to show that it could deliver at the level of contemporary social problems in ways which modern social thought fails to do.

Here the crucial move would be the recovery of concrete utopian perspectives in the context of new organizational forms. Such social thought would focus on new organizational forms rather than on theoretical radicalisms or para-philosophical voluntarisms. Thus far the postmodernity site has been littered with theoretical radicalisms (French, German, Italian) and not a single new organizational form. Such radicalisms are powerful at the level of culturalist fashion but powerless when confronted with advanced science and technology. Indeed, they may even impede adequate responses to these phenomena. A new social thought might work to relate directly to such advanced science and technology *by the innovation of new organizational forms at personal, national and international levels.*

Elements of this advance are signalled in the best French theory, albeit in a mystified, crypto anti-religious way, as well as in Wittgenstein. But the anthropological foundations for such an organizational turn are not evident in posthumanism or positivism. They go to the illusory character of modern intellectualism once it is shorn of noetic and allied to an incoherent Cartesian metaphysics of subject-object. As the late Foucault sensed, the way forward through organizational forms is an unexpected revivification of philosophical anthropology.

Discourse

A second group of implications concern whether or not the mode of discourse employed by contemporary social thought needs to change in the light of ideas or doctrines associated with postmodernity. The view that it does is open to objection methodologically and not only to the charge that it confuses French critical theory (misnamed 'postmodernism') with postmodernity. Nonetheless, it has the advantage of freshness and short-term productivity. A remarkable change of mood and perspective, a marked heightening of ethical concern and rational reflexivity, result from attempting to import such thematics into contemporary social thought.

So far the impact of such thematics has been more noticeable in social anthropology than in sociology. In France the association between social anthropologists and thinkers now dubbed postmodernists is clear (Bataille, Michael Leiris, René Girard, Levi-Strauss, Baudrillard, Lyotard). Among Anglo-Saxon social anthropologists it was Victor Turner who made the initial impact by applying van Gennep's notion of liminality to contemporary cultural change. My own essay (Hudson, 1980) on 'Social Anthropology and Post-modernist Philosophical Anthropology' was noted by British social anthropologists, although its rejection of any 'science of man' was seen as controversial. Recently the notion that social anthropology needs radical reconstruction as a discipline has become respectable, partly due to the sage-like observations of Rodney Needham and Clifford Geertz, and partly due to the impact of Foucault. In America however, a whole literature on 'postmodern ethnography' has emerged (James Clifford, Michael Fischer, Stephen Marcus, Stephen Tyler, Dennis Tredlock et al.). In this literature 'postmodernism' and 'postmodernity' are confused. Assimilation of French critical theory alleged to be 'postmodernist' is recommended as a way to make ethnography 'postmodern' (Clifford and Marcuse, 1986).

Postmodernism applied to anthropology, it is suggested, involves the end of the Enlightenment over-determination of anthropology and the rejection of the project of a science of man. The presumption of western superiority gives way to multiple voices, to a view of modern western cosmology as ethnocentric, to a comparativism of western and non-western aesthetics. Social anthropology itself is seen as *a discourse of modernity* based on the Judaeo-Christian idea of time, the myth of the west. The allegedly characteristically modern doctrines of realism, objectivity, neutrality and universality are displaced. Instead culture is seen as an inherently contested area. Poetics is understood as inherently political, science is seen as not above historical or linguistic processes.

There is a call to drop the epistemological transcendence of modern social anthropology for a reflexivity which accepts its immanence in a way which excludes any ascendancy of the knower over the known. Ethnography, it is argued, should accept its own status as *writing* (in Derrida's extended sense). This amounts to doing for ethnography what Hayden White attempted to do for historiography: that is, to win unambiguous recognition of *its literary, narrative, tropical character*. Given the rejection of representation, ethnography becomes *fiction, invention, morality, allegory*. The role of rhetoric is studied and foregrounded (Roland Barthes, Paul de Man, Hayden White); the constructive, textual nature of cultural accounts is stressed. The historicity of writing ethnography is acknowledged. Realism is replaced by attention to the partiality of the tropes and language used. Naturalism is displaced by semiotic studies of how a culture is constructed. Much is made *à la* Bakhtin of the multivocal, of the polyphonic, of bifocality, of the inter-reflexive. The new reflexivity goes with an attempt to revise social anthropology as cultural critique which serves to undermine false and self satisfied beliefs of western cultures.

Without denying the potential productivity of all this, there is a danger that doctrines recommended by cultural fashion will be taken as established and subject matter redisplayed accordingly, despite the conceptual slippage and the admission of relaxed standards of argumentation and documentation. The gains at the level of demythologization are undeniable. In so far as modern chauvinism, the myth of natives as primitive ancestors, and the imposition of western social structure as thought structure are repudiated, there are advances in understanding. There is also a will to learn from the institutions and organizational forms of radically different societies. This in turn may lead not only to cultural critique based on contrast effects, but to cultural recuperations: of the gift, of practices such as sacred dances, of *arcanae* such as arts of memory and projective cosmosophies. Such recuperations may well be doomed in advance to be ornamental and diversionary, but if the strategies implicit in them were reconstructed in contemporary practices the outcome might be very different.

No doubt related attempts will be made to bring sociology up to date with such thematics. Here much could be learnt from the growing literature which questions modernity in a French theory perspective from the specific standpoint of feminism (Jardine, 1985). Such updating may be largely agitational. In the outcome the discourse of contemporary social thought will have to change to accommodate the dilemmas to which such French thematics draw attention. However, it is unlikely to change by simply taking over these thematics. For these thematics are less solutions to than dramatizations of problems which modern social thought has failed to solve.

Social Location

A third group of implications relate to the social location of the discussion. In the existing discussion postmodernity is much criticized from a political standpoint but much of this criticism is more complicit with its object than first appears. Thus, for example, postmodernity is often identified with 'reactionary' or 'regressive' political tendencies, including:

1 the demoralization of society;
2 the dismantling of the welfare state;
3 the decimation of the public sphere;
4 a retreat into privatization, regionalism, particularism;
5 an acceptance of social disorder and fragmentation;
6 a rejection of consensus as a social organizational ideal;
7 a retreat from attempts to legitimate social and political practices;
8 a separation of politics from argumentational justification.

What is really at stake, it is suggested, is a resurgence of irrationalism, a relaxation of the standards of rationality, an alliance of the mystico-religious sublime with a renewal of positivism. Such criticism, however, does not expose most of the confusions and myths which dominate the discussion of postmodernity. It may even perpetuate them by acquiescing in corrupt argumentational practices while advancing different theses, or by maintaining cultural partitions and their social hierarchical strategies while gesturing towards democracy, equality and so forth.

To this extent, the political criticism of postmodernity needs to be examined very closely. For such criticism often has a social content quite other than that which it claims for itself. As a criticism of the 'what' of the discussion this criticism has merits. It is true that much of the existing discussion takes postmodernity at face value, that the terrain is often located as one of 'theory', as if the discussion itself was unsituated and remote from actual political, social and, above all, economic struggles. There are also merits in neo-marxist claims that postmodernity is the ideology of contemporary liberalism which, for all its pseudo-revolutionary postures, serves the interests of capital. Alternatively, postmodernity may be seen as a higher escapism centring on epiphenomenal cultural changes, while fundamental determinants such as profit maximization and the nation state remain in place.

Similarly, there *is* a need to stress that postmodernism and postmodernity can be usefully read as *interested constructions*: as constructions of late capitalist culture, as *strategies* of European cultural imperialism, as *diversions* which mask the machinations of an unequal global economy. The geopolitical realism of such readings has much to commend it, despite the conceptual slippage of 'late', 'imperialist' and so forth. But this geopolitical realism is itself often geographically blinkered, backward looking, supportive of existing hierarchies and intellectually conservative. It does not examine itself closely in the context of the *entire* contemporary world situation. Hence, it misses a crucial negative feature of the whole discussion.

This feature is the pervasive attempt to produce, prevent or influence major changes in contemporary chronopolitical historical comportment without addressing the chronopolitics involved explicitly, in detail and in an argumentational form; and without making any major adjustments at the level of intellectual equipment in order to relate adequately to the transformed situation or condition under discussion. Put as plainly as possible, the major participants attempt to chart our path into the future, but they do so from intellectual and cultural standpoints which are not mediated with the developments in science, technology and social organization of which they speak. On the contrary, despite the surfeit of political and theoretical radicalism on the table, the contemporary discussion of postmodernity is basically *a refusal of change*: a refusal to acquire the global perspectives, the mathematical and scientific literacy, the transdisciplinary horizons needed for an adequate engagement with the world now emerging.

Instead, a more disillusioned, more openly *procursive* standpoint is needed. The Europeans and their American *epigoni* should not be allowed to tie the future to the fortunes of their own cultural traditions, literatures and philosophical canons. Instead, the issues need to be genuinely globalized. Basic analytical reordering is needed to expose gross confusions and to establish workable distinctions. Until this is done, the issues raised in the discussion of postmodernity are unlikely to be resolved satisfactorily. On the contrary, abstract oppositions between badly theorized positions, positions involving claims nowhere made out (for example, about language or the subject) will continue to fill the pages of books and journal articles.

But more is required: an opening up of the social location of the entire discussion. Much of the current discussion is an in-house dialogue between Anglo-American and Franco-German philosophical and literary cultures, a dialogue in which having read Derrida or Heidegger or Wittgenstein or Adorno is much more important than understanding the world economy or having experience of famine in Africa. Instead, the discussion of a world on the move needs to be opened to that world. The 'where' of the discussion needs to be exposed and improved. At the very least, large parts of the current discussion of postmodernity needs to be displaced into other and often younger hands, towards other and more globally distributed geographic locations, to other and much more diverse disciplinary and transdisciplinary work sites. Thus, women need to figure much more prominently, and not only French and American academic women. Participants are also needed from the Soviet Union and Eastern Europe. Asia, African and Latin American voices need to be heard, including scientists and political economists and farmers and not only producers of high cultural objects. Here the issue is not populism but globalism. Elaborated somewhat, the wider social location involves a move beyond disciplinary and single art locations as well.

Once it is recognized that the existing discussion of postmodernity is obsoletely located socially, the range of issues raised by it can be subjected to a hermeneutics of social suspicion and other treatments proposed instead. The implication for contemporary social thought is that the quest for wider social location should not only take the form of inclusion or levelling. Rather, new organizational forms are needed both to make a wider social location possible, and to prevent social-locational intellectual retardation in similar cases in the future.

Given wider social location, and the new organizational forms appropriate to it, the thematics thrown up by the discussion of post-modernity may be able to be reworked in a way which does not privilege the doctrines, intellectual practices and disciplinary backgrounds of the participants so far, in a way which relates more precisely to the challenges of contemporary science and technology. Here post-philosophical anticipation, historical sobriety and organizational innovation need to combine. Post-philosophical anticipation provides the topos or site. Sober intellectual history can aid a future librarian by exposing false or premature identifications, for example in terms of French theory. But only new organizational forms, and not revisions of Nietzsche, Kant or Hegel, will lead us beyond the voluntarist illusions of a futurist history of ideas.

References

Anderson, P. (1984) 'Modernity and Revolution', *New Left Review*, 144: pp. 96–113.

Arac, J. (ed.) (1986) *Postmodernism and Politics*. Manchester: Manchester University Press.

Bell, D. (1980). *Sociological Journeys, Essays 1960–1980* London: Heinemann.

Berger, P.L. (1979) *Facing Up to Modernity*. Harmondsworth: Penguin Books Ltd.

Bouveresse, J. (1984) *Rationalité et Cynisme*. Paris: Les Editions de Minuit.

Bratu, H. (1985) 'Postmodernism Recounted: Edges, Typologies, Categories' in *Krisis*, nos. 3–4, pp. 170–93.

Burgin, V. (1986) *The End of Art Theory Criticism and Postmodernity*. London: Macmillan.

Clifford, J. and Marcuse, G.E. (1986) *Writing Culture*. Berkeley and Los Angeles: University of California Press.

Fabian, J. (1983) *Time and the Other: How Anthropology Makes its Object*. New York: Columbia University Press.

Foster, H. (ed.) (1983) *The Anti-Aesthetic*. Washington: Bay Press.

Foster, H. (1985) *Recodings — Art, Spectacle, Cultural Politics*. Washington: Bay Press.

Frisby, D. (1985) *Fragments of Modernity*. Cambridge: Polity Press.

Galgan, G.J. (1982) *The Logic of Modernity*. New York: New York University Press.

Habermas, J. (1985) *Der philosophische Diskurs der Moderne. Zwölf Vorlesungen*. Frankfurt am Main: Suhrkamp Verlag.

Hudson, W. (1980) 'Social Anthropology and Post-modernist Philosophical Anthropology', *Journal of the Anthropological Society of Oxford*, vol. XI, no. 1, pp. 31–8.

Hudson, W. (1986) 'The Question of Postmodern Philosophy' in Hudson, W. and Reijen, W. (eds) (1985) *Modernen versus Postmodernen*. Utrecht: H & S, pp. 51–89.

Hudson, W. (1987) 'Ernst Bloch: "Ideology" and Postmodern Social Philosophy' in *Canadian Journal of Political and Social Theory*, vol. 7, nos. 1–2, pp. 131–45.

Jameson, F. (1984) 'Postmodernism, or, the Cultural Logic of Late Capitalism', *New Left Review*, 146 (July-August): 53–92.

Jardine, A. (1985) *Gynesis Configurations of Women and Modernity*. Ithaca: Cornell University Press.

Jencks, C. (1986) *What is Post-Modernism?* London: Academy Editions.

Koselleck, R. (1985) *Futures Past: The Semantics of Historical Time*. English transl. Boston: M.I.T. Press.

Kumar, K. (1978) *Prophecy and Progress: The Sociology of Industrial and Post-Industrial Society*. Harmondsworth: Penguin Books.

Lawson, H. (1985) *Reflexivity: The Post-Modern Predicament*. London: Hutchinson.

Lyotard, J-F. (1984) *The Postmodern Condition: A Report on Knowledge*, trans. G. Bennington and B. Massumi. Minneapolis: University of Minnesota Press.

Lyotard, J-F. (1984) *Driftworks*, ed. R. McKeon. New York: Semiotext(e) Inc.

Lyotard, J-F. (1986) *Le Postmoderne expliqué aux enfants*. Paris: Galilée.

McLuhan, M. (1964) *Understanding Media*. London: Routledge & Kegan Paul.

Marcus, G.E. and Fischer, M.M.J. (1986) *Anthropology as Cultural Critique: An Experimental Moment in the Human Sciences*. Chicago and London: The University of Chicago Press.

Palmer, R. (1985) 'Quest for a Concept of Postmodernity' in *Krisis*, nos. 3–4, pp. 9–10.

Raulet, G. (1986) 'From Modernity as One-Way Street to Postmodernity as Dead End' in *New German Critique*, no. 33, Fall, pp. 155–77.

Raulet, G. (1984a) 'Pour une archéologie de *Post-Modernité*' in G. Raulet (ed.), *Weimar ou l'explosion de la Modernité*. Paris: Antropos, pp. 7–25.

Reiss, T.J. (1982) *The Discourse of Modernism*. Ithaca and London: Cornell University Press.

Rorty, R. (1984) 'Habermas and Lyotard on Postmodernity', in *Praxis International*, 4: no. 1, April.

Schürmann, R. (1983) 'Modernity: The Last Epoch in a Closed History?'. *Independent Journal of Philosophy*, 10:51–9.

Thiher, A. (1984) *Words in Reflection*. Chicago and London: The University of Chicago Press.

Wellmer, A. (1983) 'On the Dialectic Modernism and Postmodernism', *Praxis International*, vol. 3, no. 2, July, pp. 337–62.

Wellmer, A. (1985) *Zur Dialektik von Moderne und Postmoderne*. Frankfurt am Main: Suhrkamp Verlag.

Journal Issues

Excursions into Postmodernity (1984), Future Fall, 26–9 July 1984, Sydney.

New German Critique, no. 33, Fall, 1984, Modernity and Postmodernity Issue.

Theory, Culture and Society, vol. 2, no. 3, 1985, The Fate of Modernity Issue.

Institute of Contemporary Arts (1983), Document 4, Postmodernism issue.

Index

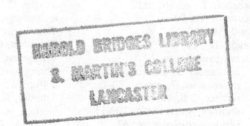